INVASION
NORTH AFRICA
1942

INVASION
NORTH AFRICA
1942

S.W.C. Pack

Charles Scribner's Sons
NEW YORK

Other Works by the Author
Anson's Voyage
Weather Forecasting
Admiral Lord Anson
The Battle of Matapan
Windward of the Caribbean
The Wager Mutiny
Britannia at Dartmouth
Sea Power in the Mediterranean
Night Action off Cape Matapan
The Battle for Crete
Cunningham the Commander
The Battle of Sirte

For Brother Jimmie,

Captain A. J. Pack, Royal Navy

Printed in Great Britain

Library of Congress Catalog Card Number 78-58572

ISBN 0-684-15921-X

Contents

Abbreviations   6

Preface   7

Under Sealed Orders   9

The Strategic Concept   17

Security   23

Amphibious Operations   27

Required Forces   35

The Plans   49

Diplomatic Mission   55

Assault on Algiers   63

Assault on Oran   81

America Invades French Morocco   91

The Assaults on Bougie and Bone   99

The Political Battle and Follow-Up   105

Abbreviations

AA	Anti-aircraft
ANCXF	Allied Naval Cdr Expeditionary Force
A/S	Anti-submarine
BAD	British Admiralty Delegation
BJSM	British Joint Staff Mission
BNLO	British Naval Liaison Officer
C-in-C	Commander-in-Chief
CCO	Chief of Combined Operations
CCS	Combined Chiefs of Staff
CNTF	Centre Naval Task Force
COS	Chief of Staff; Chiefs of Staff
CTF	Centre Task Force
D-day	Day appointed for the Assault, 8 November, 1942
ENTF	Eastern Naval Task Force
ETF	Eastern Task Force
FAA	Fleet Air Arm
FO Gib	Flag Officer, Gibraltar
GUF	Gibraltar – US Fast Convoy
GUS	Gibraltar – US Slow Convoy
KMF	UK – Mediterranean Fast Convoy
KMF(A)	UK – Mediterranean Fast Convoy to Algiers
KMF(O)	UK – Mediterranean Fast Convoy to Oran
KMS	UK – Mediterranean Slow Convoy
LCA	Landing Craft Assault
LCM	Landing Craft Mechanised
LCP	Landing Craft Personnel
LCS	Landing Craft Support
LCT	Landing Craft Tank
LCV	Landing Craft Vehicle
LSG	Landing Ship Gantry
LSI(L)	Landing Ship Infantry (large)
LSI(M)	Landing Ship Infantry (medium)
LSI(S)	Landing Ship Infantry (small)
LST	Landing Ship Tank
NCCTF	Naval Cdr CTF (Com T. Troubridge)
NCETF	Naval Cdr ETF (R-Adm H. M. Burrough)
NCWTF	Naval Cdr WTF (R-Adm H. K. Hewitt)
NCXF	Naval Cdr Expeditionary Force (Adm Sir A. Cunningham)
NOIC	Naval Officer in Charge
PR	Photographic Reconnaissance
RFA	Royal Fleet Auxiliary
R/T	Radio Telephony
S/M	Submarine

Preface

It was on Sunday, 8 November 1942, that a great combined force of British and American troops landed on the beaches of French North Africa to seize the vital ports of Algiers, Oran, and Casablanca. This was Operation Torch, an expedition which was to rank as one of the great strategic enterprises of World War 2.

Though very largely a gamble, sometimes favoured by remarkable fortune, at others dogged by mishap or bad weather, the operation resulted in complete success. It was to give the Allies control of the coast of north-west Africa from Tunis to Dakar, and in due course open up the Mediterranean Sea from Gibraltar to Alexandria. It brought an increasing realisation of defeat to the Italians, and gave to defeated France a renewed hope of freedom.

But the operation was not without considerable anxiety on the part of the Allies, who in handling the better part of a thousand warships, auxiliaries, transports, and small craft in accordance with a carefully prepared schedule and closely co-ordinated plan, at a time when there was a shortage of everything except courage and enterprise, found that they must rely greatly on good luck. This is brought out well in a letter written by the First Sea Lord, Sir Dudley Pound, to the Allied Naval Commander, Sir Andrew Cunningham, on completion of the assault phase of Torch. 'I am sure that you had as anxious a time as we did here [Admiralty]. I had visions of large convoys waltzing up and down inside as well as outside the Mediterranean, with the weather too bad to land, and the U-boats buzzing around.

'We really did have remarkable luck.'

It will be seen in the following chapters that secrecy prevailed, and miraculously the assault, placed under the overall command of General Eisenhower, took the Axis powers almost completely by surprise. The tension experienced by those in command can be summed up in Eisenhower's words. He wrote in later years to Cunningham,

'. . . the hours that you and I spent together in the dripping tunnels of Gibraltar will probably remain as long in my memory as will any other. It was there I first understood the indescribable and inescapable strain that comes over one when his part is done – when the issue rests with fate and the fighting men he has committed to action.'

The success of Operation Torch, coinciding as it did with the westward advance of the British 8th Army through Libya, led to even greater promise when two Allied armies united in Tunisia in May 1943, and brought about the surrender of General von Arnim and a quarter of a million Axis troops. This was the turning point of the War, and victory for the Allies now appeared for the first time to be within their grasp.

The author has been greatly helped by the official reports and books on Torch . In addition to serving in Washington in 1942 during the development of the decision for Torch by the Combined Chiefs of Staff, the author has benefited immeasurably by some 150 first hand accounts. From many of these he has been privileged to quote pertinent extracts. Such accounts from a dwindling number of survivors are not only valuable but are helpful in adding realism. Perhaps the most striking feature of them is the spirit of enthusiasm that prevails. There is also, in many, the atmosphere of a crusade that was felt to be the turning point of the war. Shortage of space precluded the use of many contributions, nevertheless they were all informative and the author would like once again to acknowledge each one with many thanks. It is inevitable that quotations of extracts may lead in some places to repetition, but it is hoped that the fact that they are from different observers will bring about variety and credibility.

I am greatly indebted to Messrs Brennan and Squires of the Imperial War Museum for their untiring help in the selection of illustrations and the provision of accurate captions. I am also most grateful to the Captain, the Director of Studies, and the Librarian of the Britannia Royal Naval College for assistance with books.

Above all I owe gratitude to my wife for her endless encouragement and help.

Blossom's Pasture,   *S. W. C. Pack*
Devon.   *1977*

Under Sealed Orders

The decision to launch Operation Torch, the Anglo-American landings on the coast of North Africa in November 1942, was not easily made. As will be described in the next chapter, alternative allied schemes had been considered secretly, right from the time of America's entry into the war after Japan's attack on Pearl Harbor on 7 December 1941.

The complex arguments for different plans, as seen by the Americans or the British, were further complicated by Stalin's insistence that the Allies should immediately mount a second front in Europe to provide relief from Hitler's invasion of Russia.

In spite of considerable initial disagreement among the Allies concerning what the Americans referred to as the 'overall strategic concept', Operation Torch had been mutually adopted in July 1942 by Britain's Prime Minister Churchill and America's President Roosevelt, and the vast combined plans were then prepared in the greatest secrecy.

But before becoming involved in the relative merits of alternative schemes available at that time, let us capture the spirit of the great assault by referring to extracts from various accounts by those who participated. One of the biggest problems before the operation was the requirement for secrecy to ensure the element of surprise.

'You may be interested in the following story', writes Sir Geoffrey King, 'told me by my brother Admiral E. L. S. King (now deceased) who was a member of the Board of Admiralty at the time.

'As you know, captains of ships sailing in convoy were given an envelope containing the convoy's destination, only to be opened in the event of the ship becoming detached.

'One of the Torch convoys sailed from Northern Ireland under sealed orders, but the captains were given the usual envelopes to make it appear that it was a normal convoy. One ship lost touch and the captain opened his envelope. He was so puzzled by the contents that he decided to return to port. There he showed the notice to the duty commander who was equally puzzled by the stated destination. He accordingly rang up my brother who was on duty at the Admiralty at the time, and after apologising for troubling him in the middle of the night, said he had done so because he felt there must be some mistake, as a captain had just shown him a note giving ... At this point my brother shouted 'stop'.

'Whatever else my brother may have said, he never divulged.'

R. S. Taylor writes:
'I was 5th Officer on board the Canadian Pacific vessel *Duchess of Bedford*. Some weeks before Operation Torch, we were ordered to the "Tail of the Bank" in the Clyde to await orders. After a few days, we were told that we were to be prepared for a special operation and no shore leave was granted from then on. (I always felt sorry for our 4th Officer who could see his home from the ship, often seeing his parents going in and out of the house: they of course did not know he was so near).

'All our lifeboats were removed and replaced with land-ing craft. The ship was armed with Oerlikon guns, two 12-pounders on the foredeck and one 6-inch gun aft with a marine gunner in charge. This armament had proved itself when we sank a U-boat in the North Atlantic earlier in the year.

'It was obvious that whatever was in store was going to be a large-scale operation. Many other ships, mostly troopships, were anchored around us. We still carried out our normal duties, and even when we began to fill up with American troops, mostly Rangers, we still could not guess our destination. The *Duchess of Bedford* carried approx-imately 2,000 troops.

'We sailed from the Clyde and formed into a large convoy steaming north-about around Ireland. We were joined by ships from other ports. The convoy was a most impressive sight when finally formed up.

'Some time after sailing the captain called all the ship's officers into the chart-room and opened the sealed orders he had been given before leaving. We were of course amazed to hear that we were to land troops in North Africa and fly the American flag.

'We were led into Arzeu Bay (20 miles east of Oran) by a British submarine on the night of 7 November 1942 and each ship was given an anchoring bearing. I was positioned on the Monkey Island to take bearings and report when we were on. There was no sign of activity ashore as we crept in. It was a dark night and there was a slight offshore breeze. When we were on the anchor bearing I called down to the bridge. Unfortunately we were carrying too much way and our bow nudged the beach before the anchors were let go. The landings were to commence at 1am and the first wave of landing craft were on their way at this time laden with troops. My recollection brings to mind that one soldier in our ship attempted to commit suicide just before the operation commenced.

'At first there appeared to be no resistance on shore, and the landing craft returned continually to reload with troops. We could hear small arms fire, and shortly after, shells came over from French guns. One shell hit the bridge of the HQ ship. There was considerable air activity, and our planes were going in to land paratroops at an inland airfield. We could also hear heavy gunfire from Oran, and later HMS *Rodney* opened fire from out at sea and we could hear the shells roaring over us like express trains. . . .'

By contrast Lieutenant A. Cook, destined for Les Andalouses, a bay 10 miles west of Oran, found conditions in a troopship less rugged than expected.

'My ship was the *Monarch of Bermuda*. At that time of course I had no idea that I was on an "invasion" trip; indeed nothing could have been less like a warship. I shared a two berth cabin which had a private bathroom! Later exploration revealed Bofors anti-aircraft guns, landing craft in place of the normal lifeboats, and on the poop deck an old naval 6-inch gun.

'After embarking American combat troops, and Ameri-can Red Cross nurses at Inverary, we returned to the Clyde, were made up into a convoy, and finally set sail about 24 October.

'The days at sea were largely uneventful; we seemed to sail at a frighteningly slow speed and made wide circles in the Atlantic. Everyone on board was in very good spirits; the food was excellent, far better than we had been used to in wartime Britain, although the ship had been "dry" since the Americans had arrived. On sunny afternoons the Military Band played on deck. Invasion de luxe! Other days the troops learned to chant "*Nous sommes soldats Americains, nous sommes vos amis*" and studied a small booklet giving instructions and advice on how to behave in North Africa. They also sewed on shoulder flashes of the Stars and Stripes.

'We ran through the Strait of Gibraltar at night narrowly missing the few small boats fishing with lights. There was no black-out in Africa, and sea fronts along the Moroccan coast were a blaze of light.

'We arrived off the North African coast, in the Bay of Andalucia, on the night of 7 November, and troops started going ashore by landing craft in the early hours of Sunday morning the 8th. At daybreak we could see other ships, landing vehicles and heavy equipment. About 9.00am I saw a spout of water suddenly appear about fifty yards from the ship and looked up expecting to see aircraft but the sky was clear. Within minutes there was a heavy crash; the Monarch had taken a direct hit. One officer was killed. Almost at once a British destroyer appeared and laid down a thick smoke screen. Apparently the French fortress at Mers-el-Kebir had suddenly come to life and started to shell the invaders. During the day there was a sharp naval engagement in which a French warship was sunk. About midday, some way out at sea a British battle-ship (the *Rodney*) came into view and started shelling the troublesome fortress of Mers-el-Kebir.

'PS When I look back on those days one small incident

Above left: Fast convoy KMF1 en route for Gibraltar./*Imperial War Museum*

Above: Part of the convoy bound for Gibraltar./*IWM*

Right: Boxing match enlivens the journey./*IWM*

Below: Divine service en route for Gibraltar./*IWM*

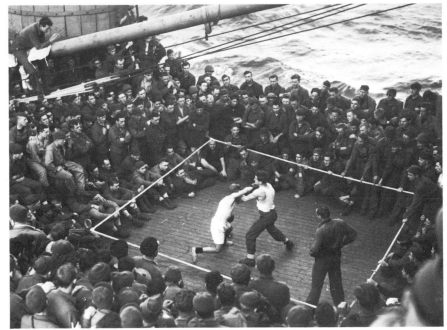

always brings a smile. On D-day in the midst of all the excitement I went down into the dining saloon in the hope of a snack. The tables were laid out as immaculately as ever; my steward, white coated, came up to me and said, "I'm sorry Sir, there's only a cold lunch today." '

The previous two extracts concerned ships that were bound for Oran. Initial ignorance about their destination similarly existed in those ships ultimately destined for Algiers, some 200 miles further east.

'I was a Lieutenant in charge of a Section in a Port Operating Co, Royal Engineers,' writes G. A. Dukes. 'We sailed from Gladstone Dock Liverpool on 24 October in the *Duchess of Richmond* (The Rolling Duchess), having carried out a most intricate journey of seven miles, utilising buses, electric train, and tram cars to convey men to Gladstone Dock.

'Security was really very good. There was no embarkation leave, and although we knew that we were destined to go abroad, we had no inkling of the eventual place. One of the cooks had been on a recent course where great attention had been given to preparing rice dishes. Even the issue of shorts was delayed until we were on board.

'The *Duchess of Richmond* had some 5,000 troops aboard, and I felt very sorry for those on the crowded lower decks. Food, however, was excellent. We joined a convoy, and made so much westing that we thought we must be bound for the United States. Eventually we found we were heading in the opposite direction, speed increased, and on the night of 7 November, Gibraltar slipped by on the port side, and the lights of Tangier shone out brightly to starboard.

'By this time, we had had sealed orders opened, and everybody had been briefed. My Company was to be landed at Algiers. I think it had been expected that we should get ashore around 6.00am, but some rather more serious resistance had been encountered, and two British destroyers

Above left: US Army Band gives a concert en route for Gibraltar./*IWM*

Left: Inspection of British troops en route for Gibraltar./*IWM*

Above: Convoy bound for Algiers./*IWM*

Right: Admiral Burrough explains forthcoming operation./*IWM*

had suffered damage at the Mole. There was a certain amount of sniping going on. We were not very well informed on the political situations, we just hoped that the French would be friendly. . . .'

Also bound for Algiers, though unaware of it until sealed orders were broken, was Lieutenant Donald MacColl, who writes,

'I was present at a beach landing to the west of Algiers on 8 November 1942. The fast convoy, KMF1, carrying the British First Army, sailed from the Clyde on 26 October 1942. I was a Temporary Lieutenant, RNVR, serving with a flotilla of British LCMs (landing craft, mechanised) which were twin-screwed petrol-driven craft with $\frac{1}{4}$ inch armour plating, tougher but slower than the diesel-powered American LCMs. They normally carried one bren gun carrier or one small tank but were also used for carrying stores and personnel. Our LCMs were embarked in the RFA *Dewdale*, a fast gantry tanker. I took passage in the *Viceroy of India*. The slow convoy, KMS 1, freighters and tankers, had sailed on 26 October. Both convoys were, of course, heavily escorted. The track from the UK was at first north-westerly making for the north-west Atlantic, then due south and finally east for Gibraltar, the voyage to Gibraltar taking 11 days.

'The assembly of the two convoys as well as the United States convoys took place to the west of Gibraltar. It was a sight I shall never forget; a vast fleet of more than 400 ships passed through the Straits on the night of 6 November, having reached that point entirely unscathed. Soon after entering the Mediterranean, two US vessels were torpedoed by a submarine; the *Thomas Stone* was taken in tow but the *Leedstown* had to be beached. These were the only casualties before the commencement of the operation proper.

'It seems extremely likely that enemy intelligence and reconnaissance had formed the mistaken opinion that an invasion had been planned for the Dakar region of West Africa; later, when their aircraft observed large numbers of ships inside the Mediterranean, they felt sure that the convoy was intended for Malta.

'During daylight on the 7th the ships sailed eastwards, apparently on course for Malta, but after dark, units altered course in groups towards their particular destinations, Oran and Algiers. During this period the convoys were covered by battleships, aircraft carriers, and cruisers of the powerful Gibraltar-based Force H. In the *Viceroy of India* we were told that our landing point was near the town of Castiglione, on a beach with the highly improbable name of Foukamarine.

'From 1.00am on the 8th, we carried out the operation of landing bren carriers and stores with no opposition from the shore; however, during the later stages of the landings, we were attacked by Italian aircraft, fortunately without casualties; we heard afterwards that a flotilla of landing craft on a neighbouring beach had been fired on by French shore batteries and four craft had been sunk. While this was happening, the destroyers, *Malcolm* and *Broke*, carrying American troops were attempting to crash the boom in Algiers harbour in the face of devastating fire from the Vichy coastal batteries. . . .'

There was little evidence of the peaceful reception by the Free French which had been hoped for by the Allies. The emphasis had intentionally been placed on American initiative for the landings in North Africa. It was thought

that there would be a greater welcome for American troops and less antipathy than that which still existed in the minds of the French towards the British who had taken such drastic steps in 1940 at the fall of France, to ensure that no French ships should be taken over by the Axis powers.

It is interesting to read observations made by Mr C. L. Harrand, who was serving in the Hunt class destroyer, HMS *Bicester*, and therefore saw the operation from the point of view of a close escort.

'5 November 1942.

'4.00pm. There have been many rumours', writes Harrand, 'and much speculation about what the object of this trip is. We left Londonderry a week ago, 27 October, and joined company with the aircraft carriers *Argus* and *Dasher*, and the cruisers *Jamaica* and *Delhi*. And now we are at Gibraltar wondering what happens next. The most popular "buzz" is Dakar. We shall soon know. It's obviously a big show. The harbour is full of shipping.

'10.30pm. We left harbour half an hour ago. All our friends are with us [Hunt class destroyers], *Zetland, Lamerton, Wilton, Bramham, Cowdray*, and *Wheatland*.

'11.00am. All hands have been mustered on the upper deck and the captain has told us we are to try and take French Morocco and Algeria; three simultaneous landings are to be made at Casablanca, Oran, and Algiers. Six large convoys are afloat, and others are to follow. Casablanca is a purely American venture; Oran is combined British and American; Algiers, the farthest east is all British. The Americans are to take the credit for the whole thing for propaganda purposes.' He then adds, 'This raised a laugh.'

The *Bicester* was to go in with the escort allocated for Algiers. Harrand continues his description of events, amplified by remarks which indicate the feelings of those taking part. 'We have a heavy battle fleet standing off land to intercept attacks from French and Italian warships.' The battleships *Rodney* and *Duke of York*, the battle cruiser

Left: The battleship *Rodney* with destroyers *Penn* (left) and *Lookout,* off Mers-el-Kebir. /*IWM*

Bottom left: The North Africa operations. Part of the convoy en route./*IWM*

Right: *Viceroy of India* torpedoed by U407 on 11 November 1942./*IWM*

Below: The last of *Viceroy of India* seen from *Boadicea*./*IWM*

Bottom: The Bay of Biscay lived up to its reputation for rough seas. Some of the convoy, in heavy weather on the way out./*IWM*

Renown, and the carriers *Formidable* and *Victorious* provided a covering force whose exact roles will be dealt with later.

For 8 November, Harrand writes, '7.00am. It is announced that US forces have landed in North Africa supported by units of the Royal Navy.' Somewhat piqued and aware of the opposition presented by the French, he adds, 'British men, ships, and aircraft: but the Yanks get the credit'. He and his shipmates obviously found it hard to accept the propaganda aspect deemed necessary in order to satisfy the American public.

Finally it is interesting to read a description by Supply Petty Officer A. Steer serving in the Infantry Assault Ship HMS *Glengyle* (Captain D. S. McGrath):

'The giant armada' says Steer, 'formed by the filtering through the Straits of Gibraltar on the night of the 6th and 7th of all units of the slow and fast convoys together with the warships forming the escort, left us with a breathtaking sight at daybreak on 8 November. It was ships, ships, and ships, as far as one could see; quite the most impressive and unforgettable convoy of all time, with Rear-Admiral H. M. Burrough, Commander of the Eastern Naval Task Force, in the combined operations Headquarters ship, HMS *Bulolo*, leading the way. General Eisenhower and Admiral Cunningham had already arrived in Supremo's Headquarters in Gibraltar.

'After dark' continues Steer, 'we set course for Les Andalouses. As we approached the beach we picked out the shaded lights of the Commandos sitting in folbots some 400 yards off the beach. These were to pilot the landing craft. Almost on schedule the first troops were put ashore. At about 8.45am, the ship's company still being at action stations, our anchorage began to be shelled by a French warship steaming round the headland. . . .'

The eye witnesses make it all sound so easy and straightforward, and it is clear that the planning had been carefully evolved so that opposition could be countered. We shall follow the planning and the operation step by step, but first to clarify those alternative schemes in the 'overall strategic concept'.

Below: Troops and baggage being disembarked from the *Duchess of Richmond*, one of the convoy ships, at Algiers./*IWM*

The Strategic Concept

At 8.00am on Sunday, 7 December 1941, six Japanese air-craft carriers had struck at the US Pacific Fleet in Pearl Harbor, annihilating most of the American battlefleet. Three days later, Japanese aircraft sank HM ships *Prince of Wales* and *Repulse* off the coast of Malaya. Further disasters were to follow, and the question in many minds was whether American entry into the war had come too late.

Churchill and Roosevelt had met at Argentia Bay, New-foundland, in the previous August while America was still at peace, and had agreed on the terms of an Atlantic Charter which, among other matters, resolved that the aggressor nations should be subdued. Germany was then the major enemy, and it was agreed that even if Japan entered the war, first priority should be given to Germany's defeat; Japan should be contained until Germany was defeated.

Very soon after America had entered the war as a result of the Japanese attack on Pearl Harbor, Churchill again met Roosevelt, this time in Washington at the conference Arcadia which began on 22 December 1941. He took with him the three British Chiefs of Staff and well prepared papers advocating possible campaigns. (His proposals are given in detail in Section iii of Chapter XIII of '*Grand Strategy*' by J. M. A. Gwyer (HMSO).) It will suffice here to summarise his plans:

(a) Continue aid to Russia.
(b) Drive the Axis forces out of Cyrenaica and Libya.
(c) Invade Morocco, Algeria, and Tunisia; initially named Operation *Gymnast*.

Thus would the allies clear the whole of the African coast of the Mediterranean, and bring about an Anglo-American occupation, preferably with the connivance of the Vichy Government, of those parts of North Africa then in the hands of the Vichy French. Britain already held troops in the UK earmarked for such an enterprise. These British troops, when released for active service might be reinforced by American troops who could, at an early date, be sent to the UK for training and preparation.

In support of the North Africa project, Churchill stressed the value to the Allies of Gibraltar's harbour and base, and referred to the unlikelihood of General Franco allowing the Germans a free passage through Spain to North Africa.

Referring to the Pacific, Churchill reiterated the pre-viously agreed policy that the destruction of Germany remained the first priority, while holding operations were conducted against Japan, and was assured that there was no intention of changing the overall policy. There re-mained, however, the need to determine what specific Anglo-American operations were practicable in order to implement the overall policy.

The Prime Minister had schemes for the possible land-ing of British and American armies in diverse places, such as Norway, Denmark, Holland, Belgium, France, Italy, and the Balkans, keen that the struggle to close and tighten the ring round Germany should begin at once and be continued remorselessly.

With the addition of America's gigantic resources now brought to bear, one might have expected great optimism

at America's entry into the war. Instead it was a time of growing concern, for the enemy were almost everywhere successful: in Russia, the Pacific, the Atlantic, and the Mediterranean. America had not been ready for war, had no specific plan, and on entry naturally wished to appropriate for herself much of the war material previously allocated to Britain. Both Britain and America were already short of adequate shipping. In the first half of the year 1942, with U-boat warfare increasing at an alarming rate, shipping losses rose to 4,000,000 tons. Such losses added greatly to the problems involved in the proposal to transfer American troops across the Atlantic for the build-up in Britain, known as Operation Bolero.

As a result of the Washington Conference of December 1941-January 1942, the Combined Chiefs of Staff Committee became established in Washington, whose constitution was defined as the 'British Chiefs of Staff (or their accredited representatives) and their American opposite numbers'. Hitherto the Americans had had no formal arrangement for

regular consultation between their Army and Navy, but they now set up in Washington a Joint Chiefs of Staff Committee: General Marshall for the army, Admiral King for the navy, and General Arnold for the air; on lines similar to those for the British Chiefs of Staff Committee in London. The term 'Joint' signified the collaboration of the military, naval, and air services of one nation, e.g. British Joint, or US Joint. The term 'Combined' on the other hand represented the combination of all the British and American services: an Allied committee as distinct from a national. The Combined Chiefs of Staff Committee was given the abbreviation CCS.

A British Joint Staff Mission (BJSM) had already been serving in Washington for some months, representing the Royal Navy, the British Army, and the Royal Air Force, largely in matters arising from the introduction in 1941 of American Lend/Lease rights for Britain: all aid short of war.

Following the Washington Conference Arcadia, the

principals in the BJSM comprised: Field Marshal Sir John Dill serving as chairman and representing the London CIGS General Sir Alan Brooke who had recently succeeded him; Admiral Sir Charles Little representing the Chief of Naval Staff, Admiral of the Fleet Sir Dudley Pound; and Air Marshal A. Harris representing the Chief of Air Staff, Air Chief Marshal Sir Charles Portal. These principals now joined the USCOS in Washington to form the CCS, which was to meet every week to resolve differences and agree on specific plans. Brooke referred to the CCS as 'the most efficient organisation that had ever been evolved for co-ordinating and correlating the war strategy and effort of the Allies.'

When considering those crucial items discussed by the CCS it is essential to bear in mind the political background associated with all military adventures. It is necessary to remember, for example, that Britain's Prime Minister had to defend his war policy in the House of Commons n January 1942, and again in July 1942, and answer criticism from many directions following some of the setbacks and misfortunes suffered in the first half of 1942. In like manner the President of the United States received mounting demand from his own people, spurred by Russian insistence for 'A second front – Now.'

The Americans agreed from the beginning that Germany must be defeated first, before a lengthy offensive in the Pacific could be mounted, and their firm view was that the Allies should concentrate on a landing in France without distractions elsewhere. They feared to become enmeshed in the Middle East war, and were opposed to Churchill's Operation Gymnast (the invasion of North Africa) which had now been renamed Super-Gymnast and envisaged participation also by the Americans.

Realising that anything planned for 1942 could only be of limited intensity owing to shortage of shipping and lack of troops trained for amphibious operations, yet aware of the need to relieve Stalin before Russia caved in altogether, the Americans proposed an alternative plan for early action on a small scale. This was called Operation Sledgehammer, which visualised a limited landing on the Cherbourg Peninsula in 1942 so as to establish a bridgehead in France which could be developed the following year, 1943.

It was clear however that whichever operation was selected, the Americans were as yet unready to provide trained troops in any great quantity for an immediate operation, and the build-up in UK (Bolero) must inevitaby be handicapped by the limitations in shipping. A further operation, Round Up, was therefore proposed, which would aim a death blow at the heart of Germany with a massive Anglo-American invasion across the English Channel to be delivered before September 1943.

There was considerable disagreement as to the timing and practicability of such operations. In supporting Round Up, the Americans, with as yet little experience of wartime transport problems and inevitable delays in the building of shipping, landing craft, airfields, military equipment, and all associated tasks, were aiming at an early date for the subjugation of Germany, realising that the Japanese must be held at bay meanwhile. The British, with recent experience of Dunkirk, and the difficulty of providing ade-

quate forces in the Middle East and nerve centres further afield, together with the need to safeguard oil supplies, were opposed to any premature assault such as Sledgehammer and Round Up that could lead to failure and permanent disaster. The Russians, however, were demanding immediate action by the Western powers to relieve their perilous position on the Eastern Front. This seemed to indicate the need for a practicable and immediate operation to forestall the possible collapse of Russia. But how was it possible to get agreement? Sledgehammer must be dropped because it was not feasible. Round Up might have to be postponed because of delays in Bolero and shipbuilding. In the British view, and it was they who would be providing the biggest contribution until America had had time to develop adequately her massive resources, considered the landings in North Africa, Super Gymnast to be launched in October 1942, as the only practicable solution. But both Marshall and King were strongly opposed. Marshall condemned Super Gymnast as expensive and ineffectual. King was apprehensive about the effect of such an operation on American holding tactics in the Pacific. He declared that it would be impossible to provide the shipping and escorts.

So keen were the Americans to obtain combined adoption of Round Up that General Marshall and Mr Hopkins visited London in person in April 1942 to explain the operation in greater detail and to press strongly for its acceptance. What is so remarkable is that there appeared to be general agreement and acceptance in London arising from the fact that the British were of course keenly in favour of the death blow ultimately to be delivered at Germany across the Channel; but not before success could be guaranteed.

Admiral Sir Andrew Cunningham was at this time in London for ten days of consultation, having relinquished his Mediterranean Command prior to going to the CCS Washington to succeed Admiral Little. 'He was an observer at the London talks,' writes Commodore Dick, his Chief of Staff, 'and although the session came to a grinding halt, a decision was finally reached by personal discussion; and an eventual draft was produced sitting on General Marshall's bed in the small hours. A paper was signed by eight men, all of undoubted good faith, which at the next stage was totally differently interpreted by the two sides.'

For those who are unfamiliar with the writing of minutes of meetings, it may be hard to appreciate the difficulties of exactly recording agreements or disagreements in words acceptable to all parties concerned. This particularly applied in those Anglo-American discussions of early 1942, when it was found that words and phrases could have a different significance despite the mistaken belief that the British and Americans spoke the same language. One thing however was clear, and that was the warmth of trust and friendship which had developed between these two staunch allies Churchill and Roosevelt.

It was during a visit by Churchill to the White House in June 1942 that he received the almost shattering news of the surrender of Tobruk; that great stronghold that had withstood siege for so long. 'What can we do to help?' Roosevelt asked, and then made the offer of 300 tanks and 100 guns. In six of America's fastest ships, the material arrived in time to play a big part in the victory of El Alamein.

The British, however, remained adamant that both Sledgehammer for 1942 and Round Up for 1943 were not practicable and could be disastrous. They were resolutely for the invasion of North Africa. The American belief was that the British were unduly biased by memories of those years of attrition and trench warfare of the First World War. They regarded the British as more concerned with the Middle East and the Indian Ocean than with the subordination of Germany.

In mid July 1942 Roosevelt sent the American Chiefs of Staff and Mr Hopkins to London with orders to clinch matters one way or the other. Discussion at Chiefs of Staff level failed to produce any agreement. Faced with deadlock the Americans telegraphed the President who thereupon decided that since the British would not look at Sledgehammer for 1942, and that the American public would be impatient to see the vast American army engaged in some operations, Sledgehammer must be abandoned and Super Gymnast must be adopted. This then was the agreement reached 24 July 1942. The name of the operation was changed again, this time from Super Gymnast to Torch, and it was agreed that it should be launched before the end of October 1942. It was also agreed that Torch should be under the supreme command of an American, a soothing of sore feelings that Churchill was keen to offer. This seemed particularly appropriate, since the troops would be mostly American, and it was also believed that the French in Africa would not be seriously opposed to an American invasion. Two days later General Eisenhower was informed by General Marshall that he, Eisenhower, was to take over supreme command of this operation with the title Commander-in-Chief Allied Expeditionary Force. It was only a year earlier that Eisenhower had reached the temporary rank of colonel. Since June 1942 he had been in England commanding, in the rank of lieutenant-general, the build-up of United States Forces (Bolero).

In Washington Admiral Sir Andrew Cunningham, as the First Sea Lord's representative, had been outspokenly in favour of Torch, and in a signal to the First Sea Lord, 21 July, he said, 'It would go a long way towards relieving the shipping problem once the short route through the Mediterranean was gained. It would jeopardise the whole of Rommel's forces and relieve anxiety about Malta. It would shake Italy to the core and rouse the occupied countries'. With his previous three years' experience as C-in-C Mediterranean, Cunningham was only too well aware that possession of Allied airfields along the North Africa seaboard would permit once more the passage of convoys through the Mediterranean: success would bring incalculable gains.

Though Eisenhower had been informed on 26 July of his appointment as Commander-in-Chief for Operation Torch, with effect from 14 August, and had nominated Brigadier-General W. Bedell Smith as his Chief of Staff the question of the naval command for Torch remained unresolved for a while. The reason was that Eisenhower, determined to achieve unity, insisted on each command being an integral part of the Allied Force responsible to

him as overall commander. His proposal that there should be a single Allied Naval Commander directly responsible to him, was questioned both in London and in Washington. Alternative proposals favoured the idea that these should be a naval officer of high standing on the staff of the Supreme Commander who would merely act as his adviser.

It is evident that Cunningham had exerted a convincing influence on the CCS Washington, speaking with the authority and experience of a former Commander-in-Chief Mediterranean. He himself* comments on the lack of enthusiasm for the North Africa operation on the part of the USCOS even after their return from London.

USCOS were also much concerned about the possible attitude of Spain and increasing liabilities if Spain were to enter the war against the Allies. Gibraltar as the great supporting base for the Torch operation would suffer considerable restrictions if it were besieged.

Cunningham's counsel, backed up by his confidence and integrity, soon won the support of the CCS in Washington, and it was mainly due to American insistence that he was selected to become the Naval Commander Expeditionary Force (NCXF) with the strong backing not only of Eisenhower but of Marshall also. It is worth noting that Marshall had a very great respect and admiration for Dill's views, in the sharing of which he was strongly in

*A Sailor's Odyssey p. 468.

Above left: Cunningham's Deputy Admiral Sir Bertram Ramsay./*IWM*

Above: Admiral Cunningham and General Eisenhower./*IWM*

Right: Cunningham's Chief of Staff Commodore R. M. Dick./*IWM*

favour of Cunningham being appointed Allied Naval Commander. Eisenhower, who referred to Cunningham as the 'Nelsonian type of Admiral who thought always in terms of attack', told Marshall how favourably he had been impressed by Cunningham, and said, 'I strongly suspect that you may have lent a helping hand towards getting him into this job.'

In London, Admiral Sir Bertram Ramsay, who had been nominated as Deputy Naval Commander, got to work at once on detailed arrangements for Torch and the preparation of plans for the amassing of the giant armada which would take 70,000 troops to Africa. The London Allied Forces Headquarters was at Norfolk House, St James's Square, and here were gathered a staff of officers of all three services of both nations.

There were to be landings at three places: Algiers and Oran inside the Mediterranean, and Casablanca on the Morocco coast outside the Mediterranean. This decision was not easily arrived at, for in addition to the strategic issue, the limitations in number of ships and landing craft loomed large. When it appeared that resources for all these landing areas might be too few, the USCOS wished to cut

out the landing at Algiers. The British view in the CCS, especially stressed by Cunningham, was that there should be a landing further east even than Algiers. Cunningham favoured a landing at Bizerta in Tunisia with the object of getting there before the Germans. He wished to make full use of ships and sea communications as supply lines to the front, and for the early establishment of Allied airfields.

He was of the opinion that a landing at Casablanca was a bit of a gamble because of the surf: the chance of Spain interfering was small and did not warrant a landing so far west.

USCOS, however, were particularly anxious about the security of such a long line of communication, insisting on the other hand that any resources earmarked for use as far east as Tunisia, should be allocated for a landing at Casablanca.

The will to agree persisted however, and with the occasional helpful prod resulting from personal willingness between Churchill and Roosevelt, agreement grew nearer. By 6 September, 1942, agreement had been reached by the CCS Washington; Ramsay in London was then able to put his staff at Norfolk House to the production of detailed orders. All the troops landed in Morocco and Oran were to be American: at Algiers half were to be American and half British. All the troops for Morocco were to sail direct from America, and the US Navy would be responsible for their transport and protection off the west coast of Morocco. The Morocco plan would be done in Washington and co-ordinated with the Norfolk House planning Staff. The Royal Navy would be responsible for the transport of troops to Algiers and Oran, all of whom, American and British, would sail from the UK. The question of naval command for the Casablanca landing caused some discussion, and was resolved by placing the Casablanca force under the US Atlantic C-in-C until it passed a certain longitude after which it became subject to the orders of the NCXF under Eisenhower.

Ramsay visited Washington in mid-September to see Cunningham and to meet the CCS. His Torch staff in London comprised Captain Geoffrey Barnard, Commander Tom Brownrigg, and Commander Manley Power, all of whom had served on Cunningham's staff in the *Warspite* during those dramatic days in the Mediterranean a year or two earlier. Cunningham himself acquired as his Chief of Staff for the operation, Commodore R. M. Dick, who had not only been with him in the *Warspite*, but also in Washington in Torch discussions from the beginning. He refers to Dick as 'a brilliant officer' who having worked with him for three years knew his methods. He also felt that Dick's intimate knowledge of French would be highly useful.

Cunningham flew with Dick to England on 20 September, for consultations but returned to Washington again on 11 October. It was necessary to prolong as long as possible the secret that operation Torch was to be launched, and that Cunningham would be leaving the CCS after only four months in Washington, to command the naval side of the greatest operation that had ever been undertaken. As part of the cover plan, Lady Cunningham had to remain in Washington long after her husband had left, to give the impression that he would return.

Cunningham's thoughts were very much on recent misfortunes in the Middle East, and the great and continuing problem of maintaining Malta, and the need to frustrate Rommel's threat at El Alamein. He mourned the loss of many fine ships in the Mediterranean but now entered with zest the preparations for a new and Allied venture which if successful would end Malta's trial and give the Allies the freedom of the Mediterranean.

Below: One of the aircraft carriers, HMS *Formidable* covering the landing operations in North Africa./*IWM*

One of the most difficult factors, and equally one of the most important, in the planning of an operation, is the preservation of secrecy. The hazards are immense, and although Torch had the reputation of having taken the Axis partners completely by surprise, it is of interest to read of some of the incidents that could so easily have divulged the imminence of the operation and the location of the objective. And for every incident exposed there must have been scores that were not.

It must be remembered that the eyes and ears of intelligence agents are everywhere, and that some publicity of offensive action, though lacking detail, is virtually demanded by the public. There is no secret about the call for 'a second front now' or the promise of a prod in 'the soft underbelly': intelligent deductions can be easily made. At the same time there is the frustrating effect of psychological warfare and the intentionally misleading role of the cover plan.

To add realism, I have reproduced below, extracts from various reports that were offered.

Lt-Col G. C. Whetmore writes: 'When the Governor of Gibraltar, Lt-Gen Sir Frank Mason-Macfarlane, returned from a visit to London in the early summer of 1942, he gave me a broad outline of the project and the role Gibraltar would be called upon to play. Among other things the colony would become the only aircraft carrier available at the out-set, and this would call for intensive administrative development in the landing and crating of aircraft, the acceptance and accommodation of growing Allied planning staff, the provision of HQ which in fact were ultimately provided in Admiralty Tunnel. He proposed an Inter Services Committee under his chairmanship to include V-Adm Sir G. F. B. Edward-Collins, Flag Officer North Atlantic; Air Cdre Simpson Commanding RAF Gibraltar; Brig Reginald Parminter, Administrator, fortress of Gibraltar; and other senior officers.'

The crucial importance of Gibraltar as a hinge on which the whole operation would rest cannot be over-estimated, and one wonders if the value of this indispensable base has ever been sufficiently appreciated. Whetmore's minutes of his meetings were sent to London for co-ordination with the detailed planning of the part that Gibraltar was to play.

Although the original intention was that the Torch landings should begin on 30 October, 1942, this date had by the middle of September been deferred a few days and changed to 4 November. There were as usual conflicting factors. On the one hand the need for making the assaults well before wintry weather should set in, and also the Russian demand for a second front now. On the other hand reasonable time must be allowed for the considerable detailed planning and the immense distribution of orders entailed.

On 26 September a Catalina flying from England to Gibraltar crashed off the coast of Spain, and the body of a naval officer was washed ashore near Cadiz. He was carrying a letter from Eisenhower's deputy in London, Maj-General Mark Clark, to the Governor of Gibraltar stating

Above: Gibraltar, the linch-pin of the operation./*IWM*

Left: Gibraltar naval base seen from the Rock./*H. Barnard*

the date of the operation and Eisenhower's intention of arriving at Gibraltar two or three days beforehand. Such a letter should have been placed in a container which would automatically disintegrate upon crashing at sea or on land. As this had not been done there existed the possibility of leakage of vital information, despite the fact that the body had been handed over by Spanish authorities without signs of tampering. The Governor cabled London, warning of the risk of compromise, and on the strength of this, Torch was postponed to 8 November.

Brigadier E. Mockler-Ferryman, from being Commander Royal Artillery, Scottish Command, was transferred in August 1942 to Norfolk House to organise an integrated Intelligence Staff at HQ. He refers to Eisenhower, scarcely known at that date, as 'a really great inter-Allied co-ordinator'. Eisenhower's Chief of Staff designate, Bedell Smith, was still in the States, but of the latter's deputy, Brigadier-General Al Gruenther, Mockler-Ferryman writes: 'He was most brilliant, and quite tireless. I became devoted to him'.

Of technical interest is the difficulty that was experienced in reconciling two languages.

'We had to start from scratch', says Mockler-Ferryman. 'The two main divisions of Intelligence are Operational and Security or, as the Americans call it, Counter Intelligence. It seemed logical to have two divisions, OI and CI. But the Americans pointed out that to them CI also meant Combat Intelligence.

'We spoke of an "Appreciation of the Situation"; they called it an "Estimate".'

' "Top Secret" was introduced because our higher grading was "Most Secret" and the Americans' plain "Secret". We had our difficulties and disagreements, but it was surprising how well and how quickly the two nations fitted together. Meanwhile, all the outside preparations were going on, high level photography along the African coast, the making and distribution of maps and training models, and a thousand and one other matters.'

In describing intelligence as a nightmare he refers to indiscreet talk by officers in bars and hotels, and the decision that the Free French were as yet to be told nothing about Torch since they had revealed a deplorable lack of security during the attack at Dakar.

'One morning', he continues, 'an officer told me that the police at Oxford had just rung up to say that a broken bundle of maps had been found on the road between Oxford and Cheltenham. As they included maps of French North Africa, the Headquarters of the Free French had been informed! I sent an officer at once to sort things out, and it transpired that the maps had fallen off a lorry. Some new ministry had moved into huts at Cheltenham and had asked the Map Section at Oxford to send them maps to cover the bare walls.'

Lt Cdr P. M. B. Chavasse, who was on the planning staff at Norfolk House writes: 'On one of the walls in our room there was a large blackboard. A light curtain hung in front of this. As a cover plan we had a large map of Norway on the board. Every morning, before office hours, a Mrs Mop came to clean the room. Of course one of the staff had to be present. On several occasions, when sweeping the floor, the lady's bottom pushed the curtain aside allowing a glance at the map of Norway.'

It cannot be stressed sufficiently that Operation Torch was complicated by the uncertainty of Allied relationship with the French in North Africa. The over-riding principle was that no offensive action should be taken against the French unless they showed hostility in which case they should then be opposed with the utmost vigour until active resistance on their part ceased. Unnecessary damage to ships and harbour installations was to be avoided as far as possible. French warships approaching Allied convoys and refusing to keep clear were to be regarded as hostile as were French aircraft.

The possibility of U-boat packs attacking the great convoys caused considerable concern to the Admiralty, who asked for more long-range aircraft to be provided for the Bay of Biscay air patrols. It was decided that every possible escort vessel, in all about a hundred and fifty must be allocated to the escort of the Torch convoys 'the most valuable ever to leave our shores', even at the risk of leaving other convoy routes unprotected.

The Axis powers had frequently reviewed their policy towards French Africa. Hitler, against the wishes of the Italians, permitted the French to maintain troops and equipment there, hoping that they would resist Allied invasion attempts. He also hoped, in return, for concessions in the use of Tunisian harbours should he ever wish himself to send German troops to Tunisia. At the same time he resisted attempts to occupy Tunisia by the Italians who were aware of increasing reports of Allied intentions to land in North Africa.

The German view in mid-October 1942 was that the Allies were possibly preparing to land in Dakar, and landings were possible in Morocco outside the Mediterranean, but unlikely in either Algeria or Tunisia. Even as late as 25 October, the Germans interpreted information of an impending operation in the Mediterranean as the preliminary to another Malta convoy. Their argument was that the Allies would avoid such landings in the Mediterranean for fear of driving the French to support the Axis powers.

To obtain a more personal and direct statement of the attitude of the local French, it had been decided in September 1942 ,to recall the US Consul General in Algiers, Mr Robert Murphy, nominally for leave in America. To avoid arousing suspicion, it was intended then to smuggle him across the Atlantic under a false name, by air Ferry Command to London where he could talk with Eisenhower and others. The meeting proved of great value, but still did not resolve what the likely reaction would be to an Allied invasion. Murphy returned by circuitous route to Algiers, where he later became convinced that the French in North Africa who favoured the Allies, would co-operate effectively if an officer of high rank could be smuggled into Africa for a secret meeting with them.

All this time intensive training for the crews of landing craft was taking place, and troops were being instructed in amphibious operations at the Combined Training Centre near Inverary in Western Scotland. Brigadier J. Wedderburn Maxwell, newly appointed Commander Royal Artillery in 78 Division which had been formed in June 1942, speaks of the division as the spearhead for Torch and the nucleus of the First Army which was to strike east with all speed from Algiers to Tunis. He also refers to several breaches of security which came to his notice while training in the Clyde area, one of which was as follows. A Staff Officer in Norfolk House was disposing of top secret papers by putting them on the fire when to his horror they were sucked straight up the chimney unburnt. They then flew out at random into St James's Square. A frantic search by staff officers to retrieve what they could, then followed. There must have been one or two red faces.

The decisive importance of secrecy was by this time understood, and it involved planning staffs in the most trying and detailed complications when working to two plans, the real plan and the cover plan. 'They succeeded brilliantly', says Wedderburn Maxwell, 'though there were some narrow shaves.' As a result, the exceptionally large concentrations of British naval forces and shipping reported at Gibraltar on 4 November were assumed by the Germans to be a Malta convoy. By this time the Allies had successfully spread a number of false plans which misled the Axis powers into expecting possible landings in various places other than those selected. Hitler, obsessed with his views on the friendship and sympathy of the French, took no precautionary measures for the time being and persuaded the Italians to do the same.

Left: Vice-Admiral Mountbatten, Chief of Combined Operations; with Commodore Troubridge, who was in command of the Centre Naval Task Force./*IWM*

Below left: Major-General V. Evelegh./*IWM*

Below: Brigadier J. Wedderburn-Maxwell RA./*IWM*

Amphibious Operations

It may be timely at this stage to refer to some of the problems implicit in planning an amphibious operation. Responsibility for developing the form of warfare which entailed a large landing of troops and equipment from the sea had been entrusted to the Combined Operations Organisation, of which Lord Louis Mountbatten was the Adviser from October 1941. In March 1942 he became its Chief, with the threefold acting rank of Vice-Admiral, Lieut-General, and Air Marshal. He was also granted membership of the British Chiefs of Staff Committee.

Besides providing advice and formulating new principles for such operations, the Organisation had to sponsor considerable development in equipment and landing craft. Implementation of new ideas had suffered however because of the more immediate need for shipbuilding generally.

Experience had shown that the firepower of modern weapons would render opposed landings on open beaches practically impossible unless some protection could be given to the assault force during the final approach from the sea. For the raid on Dieppe in August 1942 there was no preliminary softening-up from the air, or bombardment by sea, and the assault was made before dawn for the purpose of achieving surprise. The Dieppe raid was dogged by bad luck, and a chance encounter with an escorted German convoy not only alerted the defence, but frustrated the co-ordination of the individual assaults. Despite the costly and tragic failure of this raid, valuable lessons were learned, one being that fighter strength in the air was not by itself sufficient to compensate for lack of close support: co-ordinated support such as could provide vital big gun bombardment to neutralise powerful enemy defences.

The main lesson from the Dieppe raid was the need for naval assault forces to be under their own senior naval officer embarked in a headquarters ship with adequate communications for tactical development and scope for discussions with the combined commanders and staffs also embarked. However detailed the tactical plan, there must be flexibility and opportunity for immediate exploitation as necessary.

The approach to battle required troops and equipment to be carried to the assault area in a landing ship infantry (LSI) equivalent to the American combat loader. The LSI (large) could be a converted fast liner such as HMS *Glengyle*, 13,140 tons, which would fly the White Ensign as she was commanded by a naval officer; or the SS *Viceroy of India* flying the Red Ensign and commanded by a master. Several cross channel steamers such as the *Prinses Beatrix* were converted to LSI (medium) or LSI (small). The number of landing craft and the types might vary considerably in each LSI.

If the sea passage were short, an assault force could be landed on a 'shore to shore' basis, the troops being already embarked in landing craft and in position for a rapid lowering on arrival. For the long passage from the Clyde in Scotland to Algiers, which was 2,760 miles, transfer to landing craft could not take place until ships were in the vicinity of the landing beaches.

Fleet auxiliaries, flying the Blue Ensign and commanded

by a master, were required for a number of tasks such as replenishment of ammunition and supplies, in addition to special duties. The Landing Ship Gantry (LSG), for example, such as the Dale class oilers, were provided with Landing Craft Mechanised (LCM) and gantries with which to hoist them out. Sad to relate, the Landing Ship Tank and the smaller Landing Craft Tank designed to discharge tanks over a ramp that lowered on to a beach, had not been developed in sufficient numbers to be of much use for Operation Torch: those few present were found to be of great value and many useful lessons were learned, though the problem of successful negotiation of the water gap in heavy surf on a steep beach remained for some time difficult to solve.

The loading of the various transports before sailing would vary in accordance with the opposition to be expected. Though it was hoped that resistance would be light the plan in this case had to allow for the possibility of a full scale opposition. Such a precautionary over-allowance could in itself prove a handicap in expediting the next stage of the assault, the rapid advance eastward.

Because of the differing limits of speed in the sea transports, it was necessary for the assault forces to be divided into fast and slow convoys, the sailing dates to be arranged so that the slow group would leave early enough to arrive at destination at the same time as the fast group. The Headquarters Ships and fast convoy would overtake the slower convoy on the evening before the assault and lead in. A submarine would serve as a navigation mark for the approach to the lowering position which would be some seven miles from the beach.

Since a large force could not be maintained indefinitely over the beaches, the early acquirement of a deep-water port would be essential for sustaining the build-up. It would be necessary therefore to select the initial landing beaches within reasonable distance of such a port so as to make possible its early capture.

After the first wave of landing craft had been lowered and sent inshore, the transports would steam closer to the shore to speed up the arrival of the next wave which would probably include landing craft with vehicles. Then would follow, as daylight appeared, the various groups carrying tanks, guns, and supplies: at least in theory.

The question of air cover loomed large, especially for the period beginning with first light. In the early stage of the assault it was unlikely that airfields ashore would be easily captured. Allied fighters would therefore not be available at Algiers, for they could not fly from Gibraltar and back without refuelling, even if they used long-range tanks. It would be essential therefore to provide aircraft carriers with fighters embarked. No less than seven British carriers, including two fleet carriers, the *Formidable* and *Victorious;* were to be made available for the Algiers and Oran operations inside the Mediterranean, as well as for convoy defence in the long passage from Scotland. These ships would provide 130 fighters and 30 torpedo bombers. The limited scale of air defence and attack available from only seven carriers was to some extent the cause of the decision that the eastward limit of the assault must be Algiers and Bone, a decision which was taken despite Cunningham's strong advice that the assault should extend as far east as Bizerta. He was keen to occupy Tunisia as a first priority, and as on earlier occasions in the Mediterranean risk the initial Axis air threat in the hope of quickly building up local Allied air strength. Instead of assaulting Tunisia from the sea, it would now only be possible to

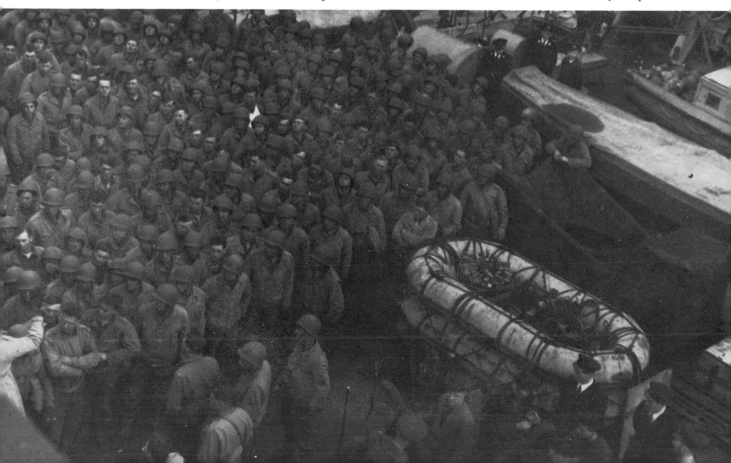

Below left: US troops assembled on
Sheffield's deck./*T. F. Mathews*

Right: Divine service for ship's company
and US troops./*T. F. Mathews*

Below: A leading seaman demonstrates a
mae-west to US troops in HMS *Sheffield*.
/*T. F. Mathews*

capture Tunis and Bizerta by advancing the 1st Army overland with long supply lines at the mercy of enemy attack.

Early in October 1942 a decision was made to employ American parachute troops to be flown all the way from England, to seize the airfields of Tafaraoui and La Senia, south of Oran, at zero hour on D-day. The possibility of using airborne troops had not previously been raised.

A further decision made about this time, and to be incorporated in the general plan, favoured direct frontal attacks against the port and harbour of both Algiers and Oran. The reason rested in the fact that harbour installations and shipping would be a full day's march from the nearest main landing beaches and there could then be a great risk of port facilities being destroyed and the harbour being blocked if the opposition so decided. However successful the initial assault landing, there would be no guarantee of continued success without a speedy build-up to follow.

Left: This American soldier relishes a drink of real Italian Vermouth on the quayside at Algiers. In the background is a dump of cork, one of the main exports from Algeria./*IWM*

Below left: American troops on the quayside after landing at Algiers./*IWM*

Right: Model of assault area in *Royal Ulsterman* with 500 US rangers to be landed at Arzeu. Captain Murray USR (left) Lieutenant-Commander W. Clark (right)./*W. Clark*

Below: A load of British troops passing through Algiers./*IWM*

Left: The first armoured vehicles landed were these American 'Half Trucks'./*IWM*

Below left: American troops moving inland after being landed./*IWM*

Above: Paratroops in Douglas transport plane en route to Tunisia from Algiers./*IWM*

Right: Scrambling nets by means of which men were able to disembark from the transports to the landing craft. Sergeant Fitton 59th Embarkation Unit RAF./*IWM*

Below: Guns being manhandled off the beach by American troops after they had been landed from landing craft./*IWM*

Above: Douglas transport planes carrying paratroops to Tunisia from Algiers./*IWM*

Right: Royal Corps of Signals Personnel in North Africa. Corporal Willacy heaves onto the cable. Driver Izzard is seen winding it in./*IWM*

Below: Paratroops dropping from a Whitley./*H. Barnard*

Required
Forces

It was estimated that assault troops in the region of 65,000 to 70,000 would be needed for the capture of Algiers, Oran, and Casablanca, allocated approximately as described below. Half the troops landed at Algiers would be American, half would be British. At Oran and Casablanca all the troops would be American. At Algiers and Oran, all the naval forces and shipping would be British; at Casablanca the naval forces and shipping would be American.

In order to prepare a workable plan for such a vast operation, which was to involve some 370 merchant ships and over 300 warships, it was necessary to begin with an assessment of the forces required at the points of assault on D-day, and then to work backwards along those routes which would be practicable, having regard to both strategic and tactical factors. These factors involved speed, size, and availability of various ships, and in addition, the two deceptive routes which would have to be followed during daylight hours in order to confuse the enemy's attempts to ascertain the destinations of the various groups.

As an example let us look first at the approach routes for the various naval task forces and covering forces as shown on Map 1.

The first requirement was for a main British force of capital ships, carriers, cruisers, and destroyers in the Mediterranean that would cover the Eastern and the Centre Task Forces and the follow-up convoys against a sea attack by Italian naval forces or those of the Vichy French. This was to be Force H, under the command of Vice-Adm

Sir Neville Syfret flying his flag in the battleship *Duke of York*. He would be under the orders of Cunningham the NCXF, whose own HQ would initially be ashore with Eisenhower in Gibraltar.

Cunningham's command as NCXF allocated to him all the Western Mediterranean, as far as a line joining Cape Bon to Marittimo in Sicily, and gave him responsibility for the safety, supply, and support of all three landings at Algiers, Oran, and Casablanca. 'The whole naval side of the entire undertaking' was his. There should, therefore, be no confusion concerning the chain of command, and reinforcement or exchange of naval forces would rest with him. (See Map 2).

In the event the possibility of using their heavy naval units was not pursued by the Italians who concluded that it could be no more than a heroic gesture on their part involving heavy sacrifices which would prejudice the continuance of vital supplies to Rommel in the Western Desert, and worsen their own already critical fuel problem. The attitude of the French Navy and the role of the French ships was to remain uncertain until after the operation had begun. The battleship *Rodney* and three destroyers, initially allocated to Force H were later transferred to the Centre Naval Task Force at Oran, to counter local opposition, thus leaving in Force H, besides the *Duke of York* and *Renown*, the fleet carriers *Victorious* (Flag of Rear-Adm Lyster) and *Formidable*, and the cruisers *Bermuda, Argonaut*, and *Sirius*.

In addition to Force H which was to patrol in the Medi-

Above: Destroyer *Enchantress* refuelling from cruiser *Sheffield*./*IWM*

Bottom: (Left to right) Rear-Admiral Burrough, Major-General Evelegh, Air Commodore Lawson, and Major-General Ryder (USA)./*IWM*

terranean north of the latitude 37° 10′N during the main assault, there was to be a Force R of one corvette, two tankers, and four trawlers for refuelling purposes in latitude 37° 50′N. There was also to be a British Force Q of the cruisers *Norfolk* and *Cumberland*, and three destroyers, to cruise off the Azores to cover the US Casablanca landing against possible enemy surface craft attack in the Atlantic.

Plans had to be prepared early for the sailing of a number of advance convoys from Britain to Gibraltar in October, comprising colliers, oilers, ammunition ships, tugs, and auxiliary craft. These were given the designation KX. Later in October the main assault convoys would sail from the United Kingdom and have the designation KM with the addition of S for slow or F for fast, and the addition of A for Algiers or O for Oran. The first *main* assault convoy to leave UK therefore would be KMS(A)1 on 22 October, steaming at eight knots. It should be due to rendezvous with KMF(A)1 at a suitable position in the Mediterranean, KMF(A)1 having left UK on 26 October, steaming at 11½ knots.

Let us examine what forces were required in all.

Forces Required for the Assault on Algiers

The 20,000 to be landed at Algiers would initially be commanded by an American, Major-General Charles W. Ryder, to give the impression that the enterprise was wholly American. It was composed of:

39th	Combat Team	(US)	4,500
168th	Combat Team	(US)	4,500
11th	Brigade	(British)	4,500
36th	Brigade	(British)	4,500
1st 6th	Commandos	(Allied)	2,000
			20,000

The objective was to seize the port of Algiers and the airfields at Blida and Maison Blanche. This military force was then to be expanded as far as was practicable to that

of an army, the British 1st Army, and the Command transferred at an appropriate moment later to Lieut-General K. A. N. Anderson. The 1st Army under Anderson, initially not much bigger than a division, was to thrust eastward to capture the port of Bougie and the airfield at Djidjelli, and then advance to Tunisia. The 78th Division which constituted the nucleus of the 1st Army had been forming and training since mid-summer 1942 and had by now acquired a fine divisional spirit under the divisional commander Major-General V. Evelegh who was to resume command as soon as the division was ashore and ready to drive eastward into Tunisia. As this was the most easterly operation, the troops were to be given the title Eastern Task Assault Force, and the ships required to take them to Algiers were to be known as the Eastern Naval Task Force (ENTF) and would come under the command of Rear-

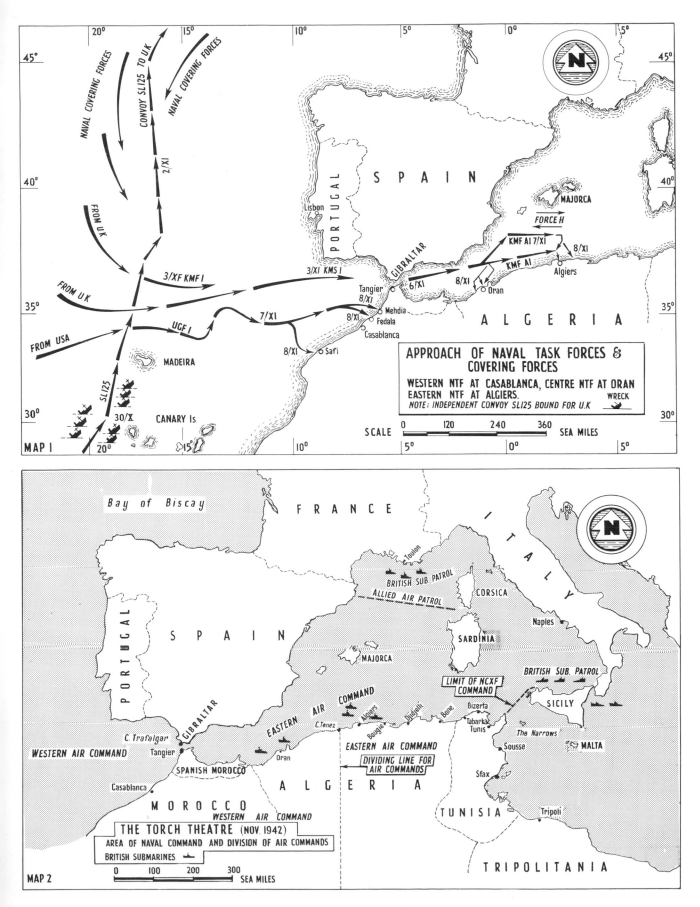

MAP I

NAVAL COVERING FORCES

CONVOY SL125 TO U.K

NAVAL COVERING FORCES

2/XI

FROM UK

FROM U K

FROM UK

FROM USA

3/XF KMF I

3/XI KMS I

UGF I

7/XI

SL125

30/X

MADEIRA

CANARY Is

S P A I N

P O R T U G A L

Lisbon

MAJORCA

FORCE H

KMF A1 7/XI

KMF A1

8/XI

8/XI

Algiers

GIBRALTAR

6/XI

8/XI

Oran

Tangier
8/XI

Mehdia
Fedala
Casablanca

8/XI

Safi

A L G E R I A

APPROACH OF NAVAL TASK FORCES & COVERING FORCES

WESTERN NTF AT CASABLANCA, CENTRE NTF AT ORAN
EASTERN NTF AT ALGIERS.
WRECK
NOTE: INDEPENDENT CONVOY SL125 BOUND FOR U.K

SCALE 0 120 240 360 SEA MILES

MAP 2

Bay of Biscay

F R A N C E

I T A L Y

Toulon

BRITISH SUB PATROL

ALLIED AIR PATROL

CORSICA

Naples

SARDINIA

BRITISH SUB. PATROL

P O R T U G A L

S P A I N

MAJORCA

LIMIT OF NCXF
COMMAND

SICILY

EASTERN   AIR   COMMAND

Bizerta

C. Trafalgar

WESTERN AIR COMMAND

GIBRALTAR

Tangier

SPANISH MOROCCO

Casablanca

C.Tenez

Algiers

Oran

Bougie

Djidjelli

Bone

Tabarka
Tunis

The Narrows

MALTA

Sousse

EASTERN AIR COMMAND

DIVIDING LINE FOR
AIR COMMANDS

Sfax

M O R O C C O

WESTERN AIR COMMAND

A L G E R I A

T U N I S I A

Tripoli

THE TORCH THEATRE (NOV. 1942)

AREA OF NAVAL COMMAND AND DIVISION OF AIR COMMANDS

BRITISH SUBMARINES

0 100 200 300 SEA MILES

T R I P O L I T A N I A

Admiral H. M. Burrough flying his flag in the HQ Ship *Bulolo*. The composition of the ENTF worked out at 92 ships of which 67 were warships or auxiliaries, and 25 were merchant vessels. The warships comprised the old aircraft carrier *Argus*, the escort carrier *Avenger*, the cruisers *Sheffield, Bermuda, Scylla,* and *Charybdis,* 13 destroyers, three submarines, together with minesweepers, sloops, corvettes, trawlers, motor launches and 25 transport. (See Map 3).

Forces Required for the Assault on Oran

The Centre Task Assault Force to be landed at Oran would be all American under the command of Major-General Lloyd R. Fredendall of the US Army. The 18,500 troops were to be composed of:

The 16th, 18th, and 26th Combat Teams	13,500
One Armoured Combat Command	4,500 (plus 180 tanks)
First Ranger Battalion	500
	18,500

This landing would be followed up also by an American force.

The objective was to land on three main beaches and capture the port of Oran from the east and from the west, and also the smaller port of Arzeu as well as the local airfields. A direct frontal attack was also to be incorporated in the original plan.

The naval force required to land troops and equipment at Oran was to be known as the Centre Naval Task Force (CNTF) and would come under the command of Commodore T. Troubridge with his broad pendant in the HQ ship *Largs*. The general plan was to be similar to that for Algiers, with the fast and slow assault convoys KMF(O)1 and KMS(O)1 meeting at a rendezvous at 4.0pm on 7 November. All the seven groups within this combination were then to continue together, as if bound for Malta, until at an appropriate moment after dark, they broke off individually to pursue their passage to the appropriate landing beaches and objectives: see Map 4, page 39. The composition of the CNTF worked out at 70 warships and 34 merchant vessels, and comprised, besides the HQ ship *Largs*, the battleship *Rodney*, the old aircraft carrier *Furious*, the escort carriers *Biter* and *Dasher*, the cruisers *Jamaica*, *Aurora*, and *Delhi*, 13 destroyers, two submarines, together with minesweepers, sloops, corvettes, trawlers, motor launches, and 34 transports.

Above left: The light cruiser *Sirius* of Force H./IWM

Below left: The cruiser *Argonaut* going alongside the oiler *Dingledale*./IWM

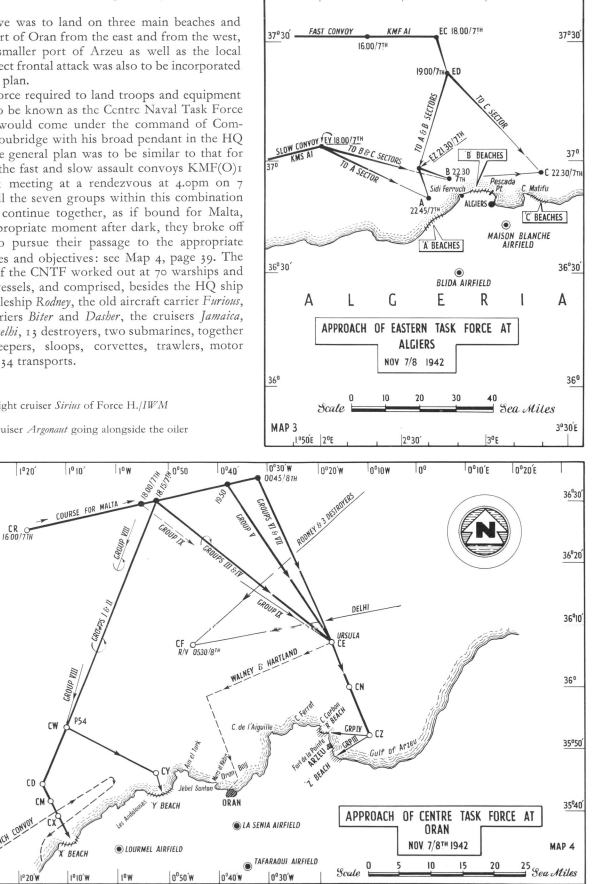

Above: The destroyer *Martin* of Force H; sunk 10 November 1942./*IWM*

Left: Force H at sea. Seafires and Martlets on *Formidable*'s flight deck; also left to right *Rodney*, *Duke of York*, *Victorious*, and *Renown*./*IWM*

Above right: Part of famous Force H lying in Algiers. They are HMS *Nelson*, HMS *Formidable* and HMS *Rodney*./*IWM*

Centre right: The aircraft carrier *Argus* operating off the Algiers coast./*IWM*

Below right: Admiral Sir Andrew Cunningham with Vice-Admiral Kent Hewitt USN./*IWM*

Forces Required for the Assault on Casablanca

The Western Task Assault Force of 31,000 American troops was to be composed of:

The 7th, 15th, 30th, 47th and 60th Combat Teams	22,500
One Armoured Combat Command	4,500
One Regiment	2,000
One Armoured Combat Team (Two battalions)	2,000
	31,000

This force would sail direct from the United States, under the command of Major-General George S. Patton of the US Army, and all the planning was to be carried out in Washington, and all the naval forces would be American.

The Western Naval Task Force (WNTF) was to be under

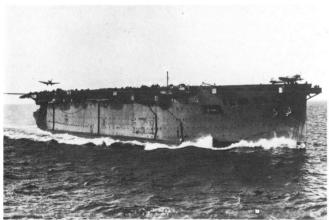

the command of Rear-Admiral H. Kent Hewitt, US Navy, who would be responsible to NCXF as soon as his force arrived in the operational area. In the preparation of this all-American enterprise the planners were spared the arguments which had arisen so repeatedly among those who were planning the Algiers landing and there is a touch of irony in the following story told by Vice-Admiral Sir Charles Hughes-Hallett.

'The American view was that the initial assault waves must be American troops owing to French memories of British action at Oran. It was argued that they were much less likely to meet resistance than British troops because of the state of anti-British feeling in North Africa.

'Countless meetings were held on the subject including the famous one when the British representatives argued that as the assault landings at Algiers were to be made in the dark, how could the French know whether the troops were British or American? There was silence for a few seconds broken by General Patton, who was sitting at the back (I have no idea why he was present since he was the Force Commander for the Casablanca landing) saying in his southern drawl the one word "*Accent!*". After that cryptic remark the tension eased!'

The WNTF was mounted at Norfolk, Virginia, and owing to its great geographical separation from the rest of the operation was given a more or less free hand by Eisenhower and Cunningham. Over the long journey there would be great danger from U-boat attack, especially in the approaches, hazards to landing craft because of the Atlantic surf on the beaches, and the risk of heavy opposition from strong French forces in Morocco. The force under Hewitt

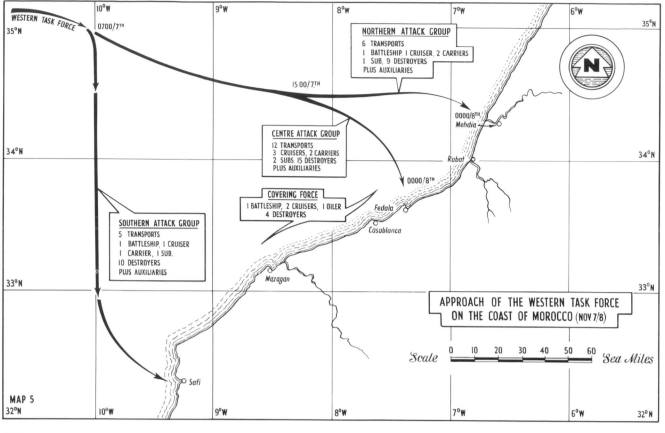

MAP 5

WESTERN TASK FORCE 0700/7TH

NORTHERN ATTACK GROUP
6 TRANSPORTS
1 BATTLESHIP, 1 CRUISER, 2 CARRIERS
1 SUB, 9 DESTROYERS
PLUS AUXILIARIES

15.00/7TH

0000/8TH
Mehdia

CENTRE ATTACK GROUP
12 TRANSPORTS
3 CRUISERS, 2 CARRIERS
2 SUBS, 15 DESTROYERS
PLUS AUXILIARIES

Rabat

0000/8TH

COVERING FORCE
1 BATTLESHIP, 2 CRUISERS, 1 OILER
4 DESTROYERS

Fedala

Casablanca

SOUTHERN ATTACK GROUP
5 TRANSPORTS
1 BATTLESHIP, 1 CRUISER
1 CARRIER, 1 SUB.
10 DESTROYERS
PLUS AUXILIARIES

Mazagan

APPROACH OF THE WESTERN TASK FORCE
ON THE COAST OF MOROCCO (NOV 7/8)

Scale   0 10 20 30 40 50 60   Sea Miles

Safi

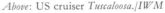

Above: US cruiser *Tuscaloosa*./*IWM*

Left: Two motor gun boats entering Algiers Harbour./*IWM*

was to consist of 91 vessels. There would be a flag group consisting of the carrier *Augusta* (flying Hewitt's flag) together with four submarines; a covering group of the battleship *Massachusetts* and the cruisers *Wichita* and *Tuscaloosa*, together with a screen of five destroyers; a fire support group of the battleship *Texas*, and perhaps another, and the cruisers *Philadelphia, Savannah,* and *Brooklyn* with 20 destroyers; an air group of the carrier *Ranger* with three auxiliary carriers and the anti-aircraft cruiser *Cleveland*, with nine destroyers; an anti-submarine and mine-sweeping group of eight; and the assault convoy of 31 transports and auxiliaries.

The WNTF was to make three widely dispersed attacks, in Morocco as shown on Map 5, page 42: the Northern Attack Group in the vicinity of Port Lyautey (Mehdia); the Centre Attack Group near Fedala, only 15 miles from Casablanca; the Southern Attack Group at Safi.

If the surf on the coast of Morocco was too heavy on D day, and the WNTF was still unable to land after waiting some days in the offing, they were then to enter the Mediterranean and land at a point between Morocco and Oran. In case of counter action by the Germans in Spanish Morocco, a force was held in England in readiness for a landing in the Tangier-Ceuta area near Gibraltar.

To each of the three Attack Groups in Hewitt's task force were allocated beacon submarines, minesweepers, and tankers. And whereas the task forces destined for Oran and Algiers were each to meet off Gibraltar their assault convoys which had sailed separately from Britain, and then escort them to their destinations, the WNTF was to take all its attack transports along with it, and divide at 7.0am on 7 November for the individual assaults.

Air Forces Required

Eisenhower would have wished for a combined air command under one commander directly responsible to him, an arrangement similar to that established for the Allied Naval Command. Such a unified command already existed in the Middle East with the integration of British and American tactical air forces and this was working successfully.

For Torch however there were to be two distinct air commands, each covering a clearly defined area: see Map 2, page 37. The Eastern Air Command (RAF) was to be under Air Marshal Sir William Welsh with headquarters at Gibraltar, and with air responsibility for the assault on Algiers. His area of responsibility over the sea extended eastward from Gibraltar; and that over the land, eastward of the longitude 1° 20′E. The dividing line on land passed through Cape Tenez, about half way between Oran and Algiers.

The Western Air Command (US Air Force) was to be under Major-General James Doolittle, with headquarters initially at Gibraltar, his responsibility to extend over land westward of Cape Tenez, covering the assaults at both Oran and Casablanca.

The Allies could between them muster just over 1,000 aircraft, as follows:

Type	Western Air Command		Eastern Air Command		Total:
	Casablanca	Oran	Gibraltar	Algiers	
Fighters	240	320	—	162	722
Bombers	114	57	—	72	243
Flying Boats	—	—	24	—	24
Maritime Strike-Recce	—	—	20	20	40
Photo-Recce	—	—	6	6	12
				Total	1,041

As the initial landings could only be supported by naval carrier-borne aircraft and the duration of such support was limited, it would be essential to seize French airfields and fly shore-based fighters in from Gibraltar at the earliest moment. It was therefore arranged that fighters would fly in from Gibraltar, 90 to Algiers, 160 to Oran, and 160 to Casablanca, within three days of the landings. It will be appreciated that the initial total of Allied fighter aircraft available for instant use, depended not so much on the numbers accessible at home, as on the speed with which cased fighters could be unpacked and assembled at Gibraltar. The requirement was largely limited by the fact that Gibraltar would become a virtual bottleneck with increasing demand for crews, fuel, stores, and unloading berths. The planned build-up was that by the end of seven weeks the total in all types of aircraft should reach 454 in the Eastern Command, and 1,244 in the Western Command.

The opposing Axis and Vichy aircraft were estimated at 1,086 as follows:

Type	Axis	Vichy
Bombers	240	185
Fighters	231	218
Recce	129	83

The tasks of the carriers would vary between bomber attacks on airfields to destroy enemy aircraft, and close air cover of troops by fighters. At the same time tactical reconnaissance, anti-submarine patrols, and a readiness to

Above right: The US aircraft carrier *Ranger* returning to base./*IWM*

Below right: Looking down on the USS *Augusta*, and in the distance HM destroyers *Zealous*, *Zephyr* and *Zodiac*./*IWM*

mount bomber attacks against units of the Italian fleet would be necessary.

Air cover for the American landings in Morocco was to be provided by 136 naval aircraft embarked in the four American carriers *Sangamon*, *Ranger*, *Suwanee*, and *Santee*. The carrier *Chenango* was to ferry 76 USAF Warhawks to the area.

Among the seven British carriers to be present for the landings at Oran and Algiers, the *Formidable*, *Victorious*, *Furious*, *Biter*, *Dasher*, *Argus*, and *Avenger*, there would be 130 fighters as well as 30 torpedo bombers. Of these carriers, the *Avenger* was to escort the slow assault convoy KMS1 from Loch Ewe to the Mediterranean, and the *Biter* was to escort the fast assault convoy KMF1 from the Clyde to the Mediterranean. The escorting carriers would embark Swordfish, for anti-submarine protection on passage, and disembark them on arrival at Gibraltar. This duty would then be taken over by the fleet carriers. These fleet carriers, together with the remaining carriers were then to proceed in military formation with the covering forces.

Having selected the forces required, Allied headquarters now had the formidable task of writing the necessary orders, and of distributing them.

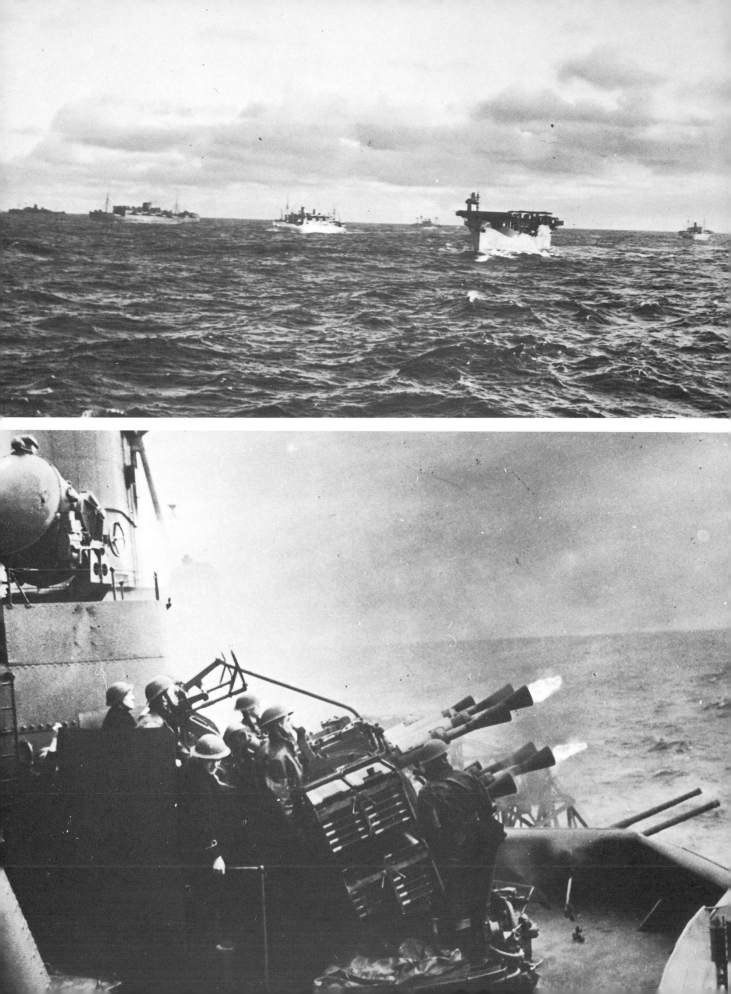

Left: Escort carrier *Avenger* with convoy for Algiers./*T. F. Mathews*

Below left: *Duke of York*'s pom-poms repelling Italian torpedo bomber attack. / *J. McGregor*

Right: Survivors embarked in the *Duke of York*./*J. McGregor*

Below: Force H as seen from *Formidable*, (left to right) *Renown, Rodney, Duke of York, Victorious*./*IWM*

Left: Allies at great pains persuade the French that Torch was US operation. /*H. Barnard*

Below: Escort carrier *Biter* in Clyde before departure for Oran./*H. Fairlie*

Bottom: The Italian battleship *Littorio* typified the potential opposition. At 42,000 tons it had a top speed of 30 knots and nine 15-inch guns./*Italian Navy*

The plans for Torch were approved by the American and British Chiefs of Staff on 29 September and 2 October, respectively, and were issued in eight parts under the signature of the deputy NCXF, Admiral Sir Bertram Ramsay, distribution beginning on 8 October. The immense and complex movement, which was to involve some 370 merchant ships and 300 warships, actually began on 2 October, six days before the final version of the plans was ready, with the sailing of KX1, the first of the six advance convoys, from the UK to Gibraltar.

The writing and issue of the plans in the short time available were masterpieces of organisation which Cunningham commended and which he says were largely due to his old Mediterranean Staff, Commodore Dick and Commanders Brownrigg, Barnard, and Power whom he had arranged to be appointed for duty at Norfolk House.

'I think Power was responsible for most of the co-ordination', he writes*, 'and I believe he dictated for about four days without stopping with four Wren stenographers on duty and another four standing off and waiting to come on. Commander Durlacher, a clever and most able Signal Officer, wrote the signal orders, which were almost as complicated and detailed as the others. . . . We worked in the closest contact with the Americans.'

The orders involved the sailing, routing, exact timing, and arrival of the advance convoys, assault convoys, and the purely naval forces in the Mediterranean, but were not concerned with the planning of the American landing at Casablanca. They comprised:

3 October
Issue of general outline
8 October
Detailed instructions for passage through Gibraltar and refuelling
8 October
Instructions for the assaults
8 October
Orders for submarines
13 October
Reallocation of forces after the assaults
12 October
Orders for follow-up convoys
12 October
Orders for convoys of ships returning to UK

The sailing of the six advance convoys (see page 50), continued through October, and it is interesting to read of the important items carried and the attention to detail required to ensure the timely arrival at Gibraltar. A rigid adherence to the time table was essential.

The four large assault convoys KMS (O and A) and KMF (O and A) sailed late in October and early in November: (see page 50). In the Mediterranean they were to divide into the sections O and A for the landings. For example KMS1 consisting of 47 slow ships and 18 escorts was to sail on 22 October, arriving off Gibraltar on 4 November at 8.00am where it would split into the two portions KMS(O) for Oran and KMS(A) for Algiers.

A Sailor's Odyssey p. 475

List of British Advance Convoys for Gibraltar

October 1942

Convoy	Size		Sailed from Clyde	Due at Gibraltar	Included
	Ships	Escorts			
KX1	5	7	2 x 42	14 x 42	3 colliers and A/S trawler group
KX2	18	13	18 x 42	31 x 42	5 ammunition ships 3 with cased aircraft, and 4 tankers
KX3	1	2	19 x 42	27 x 42	Signal personnel for Gibraltar
KX4A	20	8	21 x 42	4 xi 42	3 LST
KX4B	8	2	24 x 42 from Milford Haven	3 xi 42	Tugs, trawlers, fuelling, cased petrol
KX5	32	10	30 x 42	10 xi 42	15 coasters, 3 tankers, 5 colliers, 7 cased Petrol

List of British Assault Convoys for Oran and Algiers
via Gibraltar, October – November 1942

Convoy	Size		Sailed from Clyde	Due at Gibraltar	Included
	Ships	Escorts			
KMS(A)1	47	18	22 x 42	5 xi 42	39 Military transports and store ships
KMS(O)1				6 xi 42	
KMF(A)1	39	12	26 x 42	6 xi 42	Bulolo, Largs, and 31 LSI
KMF(O)1				6 xi 42	
KMS2	52	14	25 x 42	10 xi 42	46 Military transports and store ships
KMF2	18	8	1 xi 42	10 xi 42	13 personnel ships for Oran and Algiers

On 4 November, in positions still some 300 and 400 miles west of Gibraltar, the Slow and Fast Assault Convoys from the UK were to split into their Algiers and Oran sections. Some idea of the tight schedule involved can be derived from the following timetable of forces and convoys, amounting to some 140 ships passing Europa Point, Gibraltar, in a short period of 32½ hours, barely a day or two before the assault was due to begin. Many of the warships had to fuel at Gibraltar on the way through. Hence before daylight on 7 November, Force H, Force R, and the Assault Convoys for Algiers and Oran with their escorts, would be steaming east well inside the Mediterranean.

5 November

7.30pm	Force R
8.30pm	Cruiser and carrier escorts for ENTF
11.00pm	Monitor HMS *Roberts*
11.45pm	Algiers Slow Convoy: KMS(A)1

6 November

1.00am	Algiers Fast Convoy: KMF(A)1
3.00am	LSTs
4.30am	Force H
2.45pm	MLs for Gibraltar
4.40pm	Oran slow convoy: KMS(O)1
10.30pm	Oran fast convoy: KMF(O)1

7 November

4.00am	Carrier escort for Oran: HM ships *Furious*, *Delhi*, etc.

Below far left: Commander York in the *Formidable* indicates to FAA pilots the positions of airfields on the model of North Africa./*IWM*

Left: (Left to right) Lieutenant-General C. W. Allfrey, (5th Corps) Lieutenant-General K. A. N. Anderson, 1st Army and Major-General V. Evelegh, 78th Div.

Below left: The destroyer *Broke*, a famous name in the Royal Navy, comes alongside the cruiser *Sheffield* to embark US troops for the frontal assault on Algiers Harbour: sunk 9 November 1942./*IWM*

Below right: Captain M. L. Power who wrote the plans./*IWM*

Cunningham comments on the strain thrown on the resources and organisation at Gibraltar and the growing congestion in berths and anchorages. He felt it necessary to have a special officer to deal with such matters in assisting Admiral Edward-Collins, and applied for the services of Captain G. N. Oliver who was appointed to Gibraltar with the rank of Commodore. 'His services were invaluable', says Cunningham, 'In the event Gibraltar as a whole stood up well to the superhuman exertions demanded of it.'

The Commanders of the Eastern and Centre Naval Task Forces were to assume responsibility for the onward routing of their ships to the lowering positions upon reaching the meridian of longitude 3°W, that is in a position about halfway to Oran from Gibraltar. Burrough in the *Bulolo* would proceed to Algiers with his 65 warships and 25 merchant vessels of the ENTF. Troubridge in the *Largs* would proceed to Oran with his 70 warships and 34 transports. Further KMF and KMS Convoys were to sail at 15 day intervals.

Meanwhile the American UGF1 assault convoy consisting of nearly 100 vessels under Hewitt, and referred to as Task Force 34, had begun the long trans-Atlantic passage and was due at Casablanca on 8 November. Other convoys were to follow in a matter of days, and subsequently UGF and UGS convoys would sail at intervals of 25 days.

Orders for Force H

The duty of Force H was to cover the Eastern and Centre Task Forces and their follow-up convoys against seaborne attack by either Italian or Vichy warships. They were not, however, to proceed eastward of 4° 30′E, approximately the longitude of Minorca, except to engage the enemy. The battleship *Rodney* and three destroyers were to join the CNTF at Oran at 6.00am on 8 November, unless strong enemy forces were known to be at sea; and the cruiser *Bermuda* correspondingly was to join the ENTF at Algiers.

So much security of the operation depended on the strength of Force H that orders were issued forbidding any further reductions for the purpose of strengthening other forces. Force H was to withdraw to Oran about 13 November to refuel if the military situation permitted, and was then to be in immediate readiness for further operations.

Orders for the Eastern Naval Task Force

The ENTF was to continue its movements so as to mislead the enemy as long as possible into supposing that it was bound for Malta. It would land the Eastern Task Assault Force on beaches near Algiers at 1.00am on 8 November: H hour on D-day.

In conformity with one of the later additions to the plans, the ENTF was also empowered to implement Operation Terminal, a direct assault on Algiers harbour by the destroyers *Broke* and *Malcolm*, and could call on Force H to provide assistance if required.

Orders for the Centre Naval Task Force

The CNTF was to continue its movements so as to mislead the enemy for as long as practicable into supposing that they were bound for a point further eastward. It was to land the Centre Task Assault Force on beaches near Oran at 1.00am on 8 November.

The CNTF was also empowered to implement Operation Reservist, a direct assault on Oran harbour by the ex-American cutters *Walney* and *Hartland*.

Also in conformity with one of the later additions to the plans, American parachute troops were to be flown from England to attack at H hour the airfields of La Senia near Oran, and Tafaraoui 80 miles SSE of it. Air Marshal Welsh had strongly opposed this project, preferring to use such parachute troops and transport aircraft in the seizing of the airfields further east at Bone, Tunis, and Bizerta to forestall the build-up of enemy forces in Tunisia that must follow the Allied landings.

Orders for Submarines

Five offensive patrols off Messina and north-west of Sicily were to be maintained by the 10th Submarine Flotilla from 5 November.

Reconnaissance patrols were to be maintained off Toulon by three submarines of the 8th Submarine Flotilla. Five submarines from the 8th Submarine Flotilla were to arrive, three off Algiers, two off Oran, on 5 November for beach finding and the establishment of beacons. See Map 2.

Spitfire reinforcements arriving to give additional aerial support to the Allied Forces./*IWM*

Orders for Air Reconnaissance

Three standing air patrols were to be maintained as follows:

(a) By Catalinas from 7 November between Cape Palamos and the Strait of Bonifacio, Sardinia, to observe any warship movement from Toulon;
(b) By aircraft from Malta from 7 November between Sardinia and Sicily to observe any movement of Italian warships westward;
(c) From 3 November to observe any northerly movement of forces from Dakar in West Africa.

Air sorties were also to be made over Italian and French ports to locate the whereabouts of Axis and Vichy ships. Reconnaissance of ports in Southern France would be made by aircraft based on the United Kingdom.

Anti-Submarine Orders

Catalinas, Hudsons, and Swordfish based on Gibraltar were to act as anti-submarine escorts until the operation developed beyond the range of Gibraltar, after which the Hudsons and Swordfish would move to Algiers and Oran.

Anti-submarine patrols and fighter cover for the Assault Convoys sailing from the UK were to be provided by home based aircraft of Coastal Command to the limit of their range. Bomber Command, RAF, and the USAF 8th Air Force were to strengthen the anti-submarine patrols in the Bay of Biscay.

The Slow Assault Convoys would be routed too far west to remain under the protection of UK based aircraft, and out of range for much of their journey: see Map 1, page 37. Carrier-borne aircraft would therefore be used until the convoys came within range of aircraft from Gibraltar. Aircraft from Gibraltar, helped by American flying-boats, based on Freetown, would also cover the convoys from the USA as they approached the Moroccan coast.

Left: Lieutenant-Commander P. C. Meyrick captain of the *Walney* with some of his officers prior to Oran assault. / *Mrs M. Meyrick*

Below: Men of the Royal Engineers laying a portable metal runway on a North African airfield./*IWM*

Bottom: RAF armourers at work on a North African airfield./*IWM*

Diplomatic Mission

In mid-October a report from the representative of the American State Department, Mr Murphy, in Algiers, suggested that several French generals were anti-Vichy. With some discussion and a little persuasion it was thought that they would wish to co-operate with the Allies. A secret visit by a high-ranking officer to Africa might permit the Allied plan to be safely revealed and supported.

Mark Clark, Eisenhower's deputy, flew to Gibraltar, and then on 19 October, embarked in the British submarine P 219 (later renamed HMS *Seraph*) Lieut N. L. A. Jewell, for a secret destination in Algeria. With him as passengers were Brigadier-General Lemnitzer, Colonels Holmes and Hamblen, all of the US Army, Captain Wright, USN, and three members of the Special Boat Section, Captains Courtney and Livingstone, and Lieut Foot; *Seraph* was carrying a number of folbots (folding boats). *Seraph* slipped and proceeded from Gibraltar at 10.00pm on 19 October, and arrived seven miles off shore at a place 50 miles west of Algiers in the late evening of 21 October. At 11.15pm a prearranged light was seen inshore and half an hour later, at a mile and a half from the beach *Seraph*'s important passengers were disembarked. There was a considerable sea and swell. The first three folbots, each with two passengers, got away successfully. The fourth, into which Clark was about to clamber to join Courtney, was whipped away in a gust of wind, taken under the fore planes of the submarine, and then capsized. Clark was not in the boat at the time, and was quickly allocated to another. In due course all four folbots were safely ashore with all

eight passengers. By 1.00am on 22 October, contact had been made with the reception party ashore and the folbots concealed in the bushes. Various alarms and excursions followed, and when police became inquisitive and came to investigate such unusual local activity, the whole party had to be hidden in the locked dusty cellar of a house.

In spite of the dramatic circumstances and local hazards to both parties, Clark was able to meet Major-General Mast, the Chief of Staff to General Juin who was in command of the French Military forces in the Algiers area. Mast informed Clark that if he were given four days warning he could guarantee little or no resistance by the French army or air force to an attempted military landing by the Allies. He could also guarantee free entry into Bone. But he could not speak for the French Navy. Mast believed resistance would end after successful landings had taken place.

Clark's return from the meeting was eventful. Heavy surf, and the necessity for the utmost secrecy, which handicapped radio telephonic communication between his party and the waiting submarine, caused much delay in embarkation. Efforts lasted from 8.00pm on 22 October until 5.40am on 23 October, during which folbots capsized and in one case a folbot was swamped and lost. However, all passengers were safely reembarked by 5.40am, and had, by 3.20pm the following day, 24 October, been transferred by folbot to a Catalina for onward passage to Gibraltar.

This meeting had been very encouraging and was to be

followed by an arrangement with General Giraud, with whom Mast was in secret communication. Giraud had escaped from a German fortress prison in April 1942, and was now living in unoccupied France, but was prepared to join the Allies and co-operate. Time was getting short for on the very night that Clark and his party were struggling with their folbots in the heavy surf off the Algeria coast, the first Torch assault convoy KMS1 sailed from the UK.

But no co-operation was expected from the French Navy. Most of their senior officers looked upon Admiral Darlan as their titular head, and were loyal to Marshal Petain as the head of the French government, despite the fact that he was very much under Hitler's influence. The French Navy, with memories of British attack on their ships at Oran and Dakar in 1940, and British hostilities against the French in Syria in 1941, were much embittered, and since it was they who manned the coastal and port defences in North Africa this was most unfortunate. The French naval forces were far from negligible. Although in the western Mediterranean at Bizerta and Oran, there were only a few French destroyers, submarines, and small craft, their ships at Casablanca, Dakar, and Toulon were substantial, the only handicap being a serious shortage of fuel, a limitation shared also by the Italian navy.

Left: Gibraltar as seen from Spain at night./*H. Barnard*

Below / Right: French battleship *Jean Bart* which was attacked by aircraft from USS *Ranger* at Casablanca, November 1942./*USN*

In Toulon the French had three capital ships, seven cruisers, 28 destroyers and 15 submarines.

At Dakar there was the modern French battleship *Richelieu* and three cruisers.

At Casablanca there was the new battleship *Jean Bart*, one cruiser, seven destroyers, and eight submarines. Though unfinished the *Jean Bart* could fire her guns.

Admiral Cunningham had successfully arranged for the peaceful neutralisation of French ships under Admiral Godfroy at Alexandria in 1940, but referred later to the peculiar psychological state which continued after the surrender of France. He was under no illusion concerning possible difficulties. He had, however, developed an earlier friendship with Admiral Esteva who was now Resident General in Tunis, and hoped that if the Allies could rush assistance to Tunis before the Germans got there Esteva might be persuaded to come in on the side of the Allies.

It is worth noting that Admiral Darlan, C-in-C of the French Armed Forces, returned to France on 30 October after a tour of inspection in North Africa. He had been Chief of the Naval Staff before the war, and at France's surrender in June 1940 became a strong supporter of Marshal Petain and Laval. He had been visiting his son who was recovering from an attack of infantile paralysis in hospital in Algiers. On hearing of a relapse, he again visited Algiers by air on 4 November.

Meanwhile arrangements had been made by the Allies to effect General Giraud's escape from France and the *Seraph* had sailed from Gibraltar on 27 October for Operation Minerva, the object of which was to embark 'King Pin' from the French Riviera by submarine and then to transfer him to a Catalina for onward flight to Gibraltar.

The *Seraph* again encountered problems and mentioned them in her subsequent report: 'It is observed that the operation of transferring the passengers would have been greatly expedited had the aircraft stopped engines in the first place. We had to turn to wind and sea so as to create a lee for launching and manning folbots, and the aircraft proceeded at about one knot into the wind, slowly widening the gap between aircraft and submarine. Furthermore, the draught caused by the propellers of the aircraft made it most difficult for the folbots to approach the aircraft.

'Secondly, when the aircraft eventually did stop engines a sea anchor would have been of the greatest assistance in the operation, as with engines stopped the aircraft drifted to leeward nearly as fast as the folbots could proceed through water.'

However 'King Pin' was safely transferred to the Catalina which arrived at Gibraltar on the eve of D-day. It was hoped that his great influence would unite the many divergent factions in Africa and end any opposition to the Anglo-American landings. In fact he flatly declined to take any part in Torch except as Supreme Commander insisting at the same time that a major part of the convoy should be diverted for landing in the south of France.

In the meantime Cunningham had taken passage from Plymouth to Gibraltar in the cruiser *Scylla*, leaving his deputy, Admiral Ramsay, in London to act as his rear link and with direct access to the Admiralty. With him in the *Scylla* were his Chief of Staff Commodore Dick, Secretary Captain Shaw, and Flag Lieutenant Dampier. On disembarking on 1 November, they were offered accommodation at the Mount by Flag Officer, Gibraltar, Admiral Edward-Collins. Eisenhower was to fly to Gibraltar on

5 November, and was accommodated at the Convent, the Residence of the Governor, Lieutenant-General Sir Frank Mason-Macfarlane.

'We had plenty to do', Cunningham writes, 'in installing ourselves in our offices in the tunnel burrowed into the Rock.' He remarks on the fact that the Supreme Commander's offices were close to his and that there was a combined Naval and Royal Air Force operations room, and mentions the 'outstandingly fine work' of the RAF working from their very congested airfield on the North Front.

'On the large wall charts in the operations room', he continues, 'we anxiously watched the progress of the convoy, now all at sea and coming through the Atlantic. German submarines had lately been very active and the losses of merchant vessels heavy, partly owing to the reduction of escorts which had been withdrawn to protect the Torch convoys.'

The return of Darlan to Algiers on 4 November, altered dramatically the political situation, and so far as could be judged at the time could prejudice the chances of French

Above left: Survivors in *Zetland* after the *Broke* had sunk./N. *Twigge*

Left: *Zetland* taking off *Broke* survivors./N. *Twigge*

Below left: *Broke* listing heavily./N. *Twigge*

Below: The end of the gallant *Broke*./N. *Twigge*

Right: Lieutenant Wickham directing operations in *Zetland*./N. *Twigge*

Below right: *Broke's* last moments./N. *Twigge*

collaboration. General Giraud's arrival at Gibraltar on 7 November did little to improve the outlook.

Brigadier Mockler-Ferryman writes of his own flight to Gibraltar with various members of his Intelligence Staff in 'six Flying Fortresses, crossing the Bay of Biscay at wave height. One of the six was intercepted in the Bay and sprayed with bullets. We landed on the tiny airstrip at Gibraltar which was already packed tight with fighters.' He mentions Giraud's arrival in the tunnel.

'Giraud,' he continues, 'was a hero of the first War. We watched him walking along the tunnel to Eisenhower's room. There was a long and difficult conference during which Giraud made frequent use of the words 'pride' and 'prestige'; in short he expected to be the Allied Commander-in-Chief, and was not in a mood for compromise. Next day, however, he accepted the offer to be C-in-C of all the French forces in North Africa against Axis aggression.'

Cunningham regarded Giraud as out of date and also unaware of the enormous preparation that had been required to launch such a vast amphibious operation as Torch. It was after a meeting at Government House, Gibraltar, on the morning of 8 November, to which Cunningham took Dick his Chief of Staff who was fluent in French, that 'Giraud finally came off his high horse . . . and declared himself willing to co-operate.' It was early that morning that the British submarine *Sybil* had embarked Giraud's staff off shore near Toulon, following which she was ordered to take them to Algiers.

Matters, however, were looking much brighter. Only a few days earlier on 3 November came the welcome news that the Eighth Army had completed its great stroke at El Alamein. By 5 November the British were advancing along the whole front, and on the 6th came news from Montgomery that the Battle of El Alamein had ended in complete and absolute victory. Seldom can there have been a more welcome signal: 'The Axis Forces are in full retreat': a wonderful augury on the eve of the great Torch landings.

Left: Troops embarked in *Sheffield*. /*A. M. Lucas*

Below left: Troops in *Sheffield* prior to transfer to *Broke* and *Malcolm*./*A. M. Lucas*

Right: Ships, escorted by aircraft from Gibraltar, discharging troops and equipment off Algiers./*P. Dyer*

Below: An Albacore taking off from *Formidable*./*IWM*

Above: HMS *Broke* after transference of troops./*A. M. Lucas*

Left: Twilight landing at Sidi Ferruch.
/ *P. Dyer*

Assault on Algiers

The biggest menace to the vast Torch armada was the threat of hostile submarines that might be met on passage. Some idea of the wealth of targets presented to them in the Western Approaches between the UK and the Azores/Gibraltar latitude, can be seen in Map 1, page 37, which shows parts of the tracks of the covering forces and those of the assault convoys with their escorts.

The warship sailings began with the departure of the carrier *Furious* and three destroyers from the Clyde on 20 October, to be followed by the battleship *Rodney* and three destroyers from Scapa on 23 October. Both groups were later to join the CNTF for the assault on Oran.

On 27 October the carriers *Argus* and *Dasher*, with the cruisers *Jamaica* and *Delhi*, and four escorts, sailed from the Clyde, followed on 30 October by Force H, the heavy covering force, comprising the battleship *Duke of York*, battle cruiser *Renown*, the cruiser *Argonaut*, and eight destroyers from Scapa, and the armoured carriers *Formidable* and *Victorious* with eight destroyers from the Clyde.

It is known that the German High Command became aware during October of the increased activity in British ports, and realised that a large expeditionary force was about to be sent overseas. They concluded however, that the blow would be directed at Dakar, and so made their dispositions accordingly, some 60 U-boats being massed around the Azores and Madeira, in addition to large numbers further north in the latitudes 45° to 50°.

Several chance sightings were made and reported by enemy aircraft and by U-boats between 26 October and 3 November, and the fact that all the naval groups completed the ocean passage in safety, speaks well for the effectiveness of the considerable anti-submarine and anti-aircraft measures. Such immunity was largely due to the Allied aircraft keeping shadowers away, and forcing U-boats to remain submerged for long periods. But perhaps the most outstanding factor in their preservation was the fortuitous passage of a large homeward bound convoy SL125 which passed to the north and east of the invasion fleet. See Map 1, page 37. This convoy comprised 42 vessels which had sailed from Sierra Leone and which became the immediate target for a pack of U-boats that turned in pursuit of SL125 as soon as it was sighted and reported. In attacks lasting four consecutive nights the U-boats sank 13 ships of convoy SL125 as it meandered northward from a position 1,000 miles south-westward of Gibraltar on 26 October to a point 600 miles westward of Gibraltar on 31 October. Following this long chase however, the U-boats left the route to Gibraltar quite clear for the oncoming invasion convoys KMS1, KMS2, and KMF1, who then miraculously slipped through these historic waters without harm. It was here that Rooke had seized Gibraltar in 1704; Rodney had fought the Moonlight Battle to relieve the great fortress in 1780. An impressive array of names of British admirals comes to mind, and a memory that in 1796 Britain had had to withdraw her ships altogether from the Mediterranean. It was not until early 1798 that a British squadron entered that sea

positions off Algiers. See Map 3, page 39. There was a moderate north-east breeze, slight sea, and good visibility. Coast lights were burning. To seaward of the landing ships, the escorts kept up a constant anti-submarine patrol while the ships approached their respective sectors A, B, and C, each identified by the beacon submarines that were to indicate the correct lowering positions. Unfortunately an unexpected set of nearly four knots to the west existed in B sector and this caused some ships to drift to the westward of their intended lowering positions. It also resulted in many of those troops earmarked for the B sector, landing instead in the A sector.

The landing beaches extended for a distance roughly 40 miles along the coast, there being from west to east, two beaches in the A sector covering five miles of coastline, six beaches in B sector covering 12 miles, and five in C sector covering five miles. This left unattended for the moment, a five mile gap between A and B sectors; also, the whole of Algiers Bay as a 13 mile gap between B and C sectors. A, B, and C beaches were further subdivided from west to east as follows:

A – Green and White;
B – Green, White, Red 1, Red 2, Red 3, and Red 4;
C – Queenie Red, Charlie Green, Charlie Blue, Charlie Red 1, and Charlie Red 2.

It is of interest to read of the feelings and reactions of some of those present. John McConnell, a supply assistant in the Dutch LSI *Marnix* reveals the picture of a less publicised angle of a night attack.

'All ships', he writes, 'were declared "dry". This news wasn't received with much enthusiasm by the naval party, and the enforced rum abstinence lasted until the night of the landings. We were in a Dutch vessel along with what seemed to be thousands of infantrymen from the East Surreys and Royal West Kents. At around 8.00pm on the night of the landings, a rum issue was started. The spirit was served, mixed with water, to all on board, and Warrant Officer Gunners witnessed the issue. The first two witnessing officers having "tested for salt" a little too often, had to be put to bed. Charitably this was regarded as due to "inhaling the rum fumes" though the Supply Chief Petty Officer survived the whole issue. Not a few sailors spent the night in cells.

'The unexpected bonus of rum went down very well with the infantry lads. It certainly relieved their tensions, and as each crowded LCA (Landing Craft, Assault) pulled away from the parent ship, the night was loud with barrack room ballads.'

It can be imagined that tensions would soon return, when the order for silence was passed round and the serious business of approaching the beaches took place. General Ryder had only that afternoon repeated an earlier assess-

again, led by Nelson. His annihilating victory at the Battle of the Nile came a few months later on 1 August 1798. In like manner, Cunningham, regarded by many as a second Nelson, was now commanding task forces which in combined efforts by land, sea, and air, were to wrest control of this sea, and gain the Allies freedom of manoeuvre.

By the evening of 7 November the heavy forces and assault convoys were well inside the Mediterranean, poised at appropriate rendezvous off Oran and off Algiers: see Map 1.

Their courses all day, until dusk at about 6.00pm, had been such as to indicate a destination further eastward, rather than the Algerian coast. The only casualty had been the American combat loader *Thomas C. Stone* in KMF1, torpedoed at 6.50am that morning by a U-boat, with the loss of nine lives. She was stopped but at once taken in tow. 'When she eventually arrived in tow off Algiers four days later', writes Chavasse, 'she herself was towing a landing craft astern. Admiral Burrough made the signal "Who is pulling, and who is pushing?" '

As Admiral Burrough's Eastern Naval Task Force passed through the various planned positions, they divided and redivided so as to arrive at the respective lowering

ment that although resistance by French and Army units might be slight, the French naval forces would put up a fight, using harbour defences to the full. Also in the HQ ship *Bulolo* with Admiral Burrough and General Ryder was General Evelegh whose operational command of the 78th Division was to begin after the landings had been completed.

At 6.00pm on 7 November, in accordance with the plans KMF(A)1, then being in a position 45 miles north of Algiers, and the sun having set an hour beforehand, Admiral Burrough in the *Bulolo* wheeled his Algiers fast convoy to the south: see Map 3. At this moment his slow convoy, KMS(A)1 had reached a position 45 miles west-north-west of the A sector beaches, till then steaming as if for Malta. They now divided into two groups, one bound for a rendezvous about seven miles off the A sector beach, the other bound for rendezvous B about seven miles off the B sector beach. They reached positions A and B at 10.14pm and 10.20pm respectively. Meanwhile the fast convoy

proceeding south, at 7.0pm divided into two groups, one group making for the A and B sectors, there to join with some of the slow convoy; the other group making for position C which was seven miles off the C sector beaches.

In each sector the submarines marking the release positions were in place and homing arrangements worked well. Burrough in the *Bulolo* had under his command some 30 ships for the landings in the three sectors, together with the smaller warships of the close escort. Also under his command were the warships of the covering force, comprising the cruisers *Sheffield, Scylla, Charybdis,* the carriers *Argus* and *Avenger,* and the monitor *Roberts.*

Within a matter of minutes of the appointed times, the

Below: Transports lying off Algiers./*IWM*

Bottom: Landing vehicles and guns at a beach near Algiers. Note small native, bottom left./*IWM*

The submarine then moved to her inner beacon position, two miles from A beach Green. A folbot with a flashing light was also in position 400 yards from the beach.

The first flight of LCAs from the *Karanja* arrived punctually at H hour, 1.00am on the 8th. These were followed by a second flight five minutes later; and in yet another five minutes, *Viceroy*'s flotilla was landed. The *Marnix* lowered all her landing craft which then, owing to the swinging of the ship, closed a destroyer instead of the motor launch that was to lead them in. Despite this, they found the correct beach, A white, and successfully landed the assault wave of the Northamptons.

In the *Karanja* was Captain R. C. Taylor, of B Company 1st Battalion the East Surrey Regiment. He writes,

'War is always strange, but surely one of its strangest aspects must be the extraordinary contrast of leaving a warm, luxurious cabin, for the dangers of landing on a hostile shore. Now was the moment of truth. First my webbing equipment and water bottle, then pistol, binoculars, ammunition, grenades (Nos 36 and 39) spare anti-tank mine, anti-gas cape, small pack with the 48 hour rations, wire cutters, toggle rope, mae west, steel helmet; all was gradually draped on or around me. I staggered under the weight, yet I was supposed to rush ashore like that to engage the enemy.

'The Company Commander (Buchanan) put his head round the door. "Could you carry a spare tin of peach slices?" "Yes I could, but it would have to be inside my battle-dress blouse." I was now all set to invade North Africa.

'We all had a rum ration before getting into our LCAs. As the sea was somewhat choppy my 30 men were promptly sea sick and the fumes all but overpowering.

'A quarter of a mile from shore we hit the only rocks for miles around. As my LCA struck we prepared to leap out in the approved manner. The first men almost disappeared. In fact the water was about 5ft deep, and one of my men was supposed to be pushing the company bicycle. As we came ashore I can still recall the sight of our company runner emerging from the sea. First only his head showing, then at last the bicycle coming through the waves.

'When we were about a mile inland we could still hear

landing ships were stopped and in position ready to go to landing stations. In the A sector were the *Karanja* (Brigade HQ and East Surreys), *Viceroy of India* (Lancashire Fusiliers), and the Dutch *Marnix* (Northamptons and Royal West Kents). The Senior Naval Officer Landings (SNOL) in this sector was Captain N. V. Dickinson who quickly supervised the transfer of pilots from submarine P 221 to the motor launches that would lead in to the A beaches.

the shouts and oaths of the sailors on the beach trying to sort things out. One hostile Frenchman, with a rifle, could have ... but luckily there were none. To find exactly where we were, we eventually stopped an Arab driving a donkey and cart in the early light. He was somewhat surprised at the sight of a hundred or so sea-soaked soldiers, but seemed quite happy to direct us to our final objectives – at Fouka and the lighthouse at Fouka Marine.'

Below: British troops landing on beach near Algiers./*IWM*

Top left: Commodore J. A. V. Morse in charge of berthing and docking at Algiers./*IWM*

Above left: Lieutenant B. H. C. Nation who captured Blida airfield with a handful of FAA Martlets from the carrier *Victorious*./*IWM*

Top: Landing craft leaving transports at Algiers./*IWM*

Above: General view of Algiers./*IWM*

Homed by submarine P 48, release position B was reached at 10.20pm by Burrough in the *Bulolo*, together with destroyer and small craft close escort, and the landing ships *Keren, Winchester Castle, Otranto, Sobieski, Awatea, Strathnaver*, and *Cathay*. These were carrying the 168th Combat Team, Commandos, and a floating reserve of the 36th Infantry Brigade, besides 77 landing craft of various kinds. With them were the 11 transports of the KMS(A)1 portion carrying between them 31 medium landing craft and stores. SNOL for B sector was Captain R. J. Shaw.

Mainly because of the strong set to westward, the procedure for landing in the B sector partly broke down. The pilot from the submarine was not picked up, with the result that the flights from the *Keren* and *Awatea*, with the exception of two craft, landed too far to the westward, causing great congestion. Those who landed at Sidi Ferruch Point were successful in capturing the fort, whose commander later obligingly arranged for buses to take them to the airfield at Blida, but warned them that the French there might fight. The airfield at Maison Blanche was captured between 6.00am and 6.30am. And soon after 9.00am, RAF fighters from Gibraltar had landed at Maison Blanche, but through scarcity of fuel many were unable to fly until the following day. It is fortunate that little opposition was met on the beaches, nevertheless six landing craft in the B·Red area were fired upon by the Ilot de la Marine in the Bay of Algiers, and four of those were sunk.

A note from Captain H. Hodge, RA, TD, who was in the *Otranto* says: 'Most of our Regiment (58th Kent) arrived off Sidi Ferruch and after the first wave of Commandos and American Rangers had landed to capture Maison Blanche Airport we were stationary (targets!) for the hours of daylight of 8 November. Such a calm sea all day. At night when we were sent to our various "sally" ports the waves were 10ft high. It is quite an experience to go from bright lights through a blanket curtain into darkness – down a short ladder (wearing full kit) and jump into darkness at the command of someone from the landing craft.

'There was no resistance on the beach and very soon our Regiment was on the 17 mile march to Algiers. It was noticeable that on this journey we passed American units brewing up coffee.

'Firing was heard mostly in the rear and we arrived finally at some army barracks in El Biar. Later that night we took over the tramway depot at El Biar and (this you won't believe!) we sent out from RHQ a call for tram drivers. A versatile lot the 58th – by morning the drivers and gunners went slowly down the winding hill from El Biar to Algiers port and returned towing the Regimental guns. These were soon deployed to give AA protection for Algiers.

'There are sad memories of members of the Regiment who took ship further East to Bone and were lost en route by torpedo action.'

The ships bound for position C for the landings in C sector arrived there at 9.35pm and were immediately sighted by the beacon submarine P 45 as their screening

Above left: Minesweepers in harbour./*IWM*

Left: Fire support for the Centre Attack Group, Western Naval Task Force, US cruiser *Augusta* and US auxiliary carrier *Charger*./*USNI*

Above: Weapons and equipment being landed on the beach preparatory to the assault on the aerodrome./*IWM*

Right: Airborne troops discuss the situation with a member of the Tank Corps./*IWM*

destroyers and minesweepers approached. Besides the close escort this group comprised the fast combat loaders *Samuel Chase, Leedstown,* and *Almaack.* Soon after the sighting of the combat loaders, the pilots from P 45 went on board the *Samuel Chase* when a conference was held with the SNOL C Sector, Captain C. D. Edgar, and the Military Commander. Some amendments were made so as to advance the release of the first flight of landing craft by half an hour; but this amendment failed to reach all concerned, with the result that men intended for both the Blue and Red beaches in C sector, all landed on Blue beach. Part of the 1st Commando were landed on Green beach by the *Leedstown* landing craft at 2.50am, nearly two hours late. Their task was to attack the batteries at Cape Matifou which at 3.40am opened fire on ships operating off shore. By this time ships were moving in closer to the beaches, and the ferry service to the shore was working satisfactorily. HMS *Zetland*, a Hunt Class destroyer supporting C sector, immediately replied and extinguished a troublesome searchlight. Stubborn resistance from Matifou continued at times but was finally silenced that afternoon by the cruiser

Above left: A general view showing RAF and American 'Task' troops being landed at Surcouf about 20 miles east of Algiers./*IWM*

Left: American troops driving away in Jeeps after being landed in landing craft./*IWM*

Top: Headed by 'Old Glory' these American troops set off for Maison Blanche aerodrome which was soon in their possession./*IWM*

Above: The first French prisoners who were taken by the Americans./*IWM*

Right: Men of an RAF regiment marching inland to take possession of Maison Blanche aerodrome./*IWM*

Bermuda and bombers from the carriers. Colonel B. G. B. Pugh writes,

'Briefly, I was at the time adjutant of No 1 Commando, reinforced for the operation by four American Troops, one half being carried in the *Otranto* for B sector and the other half in the *Leedstown* for C sector. Their task was to capture the two coast defence batteries to the west and east of the Bay of Algiers; Sidi Ferruch and Cape Matifou. The landing at the former place was unopposed, which was lucky, as a couple of the LCAs broached to and capsized on the beach. The fort was handed over to us without any incident or shot being fired.

'The landing at Cape Matifou was also unopposed but the garrison at Fort d'Estrées nearby put up some stout resistance which took half a day's skirmishing to quell. We unfortunately had a number of casualties there.'

At 1.40am Burrough ordered the destroyers *Broke* (Lt Cdr A. F. C. Layard) and *Malcolm* (Cdr A. B. Russell) to carry out operation Terminal under the command of Captain H. St J. Fancourt, in accordance with the plan to prevent the French from scuttling ships and demolishing harbour installations. This was intended as a frontal assault on the harbour itself, the ships to enter the southern entrance, and upon securing alongside the Quai de Dieppe (just one of some 30 jetties) to be prepared to land three companies of American troops.

The *Broke* at once led off from position B on her 20 mile circuitous journey to the port of Algiers, keeping five miles to seaward of the B sector beaches, with *Malcolm* following a mile astern.

At 3.45am the *Broke* and *Malcolm* were in the vicinity of the southern entrance, but failed to find it, owing to the dark background of hills, the dazzle of searchlights, and troublesome gunfire. A further attempt was made, this time using starshell, but again without success. At 4.07am

the *Malcolm* was hit and received such heavy boiler room damage that she was forced to withdraw.

Meanwhile the *Broke* made a further attempt, but again without finding the entrance. At her fourth attempt however, at 5.20am, as dawn was breaking, success crowned her efforts. She charged the boom at full speed, smoothly and effectively, and proceeded towards a jetty 600 yards ahead on her port bow. A French minesweeper opened fire on her, wounding the *Broke*'s coxswain as he steered alongside. Troops were landed and the nearby power station and oil installations were secured. For some time, apart from sniping and machine gun fire, conditions were fairly satisfactory, but the *Broke* had to shift berth twice during the next two hours to attain shelter, especially from the harbour battery at the northern entrance about a mile away. Cross fire also developed, though no attempt was made to sabotage shipping in the harbour. Fancourt therefore, recalled some of the boarding party in preparation for a hasty exit.

By 9.15am *Broke* was under attack from a new quarter. This fire was well controlled and three shells narrowly missed her. Fancourt reluctantly decided to withdraw the *Broke* from harbour and issued the general recall of troops from the shore. As she moved across the harbour the *Broke* was hit repeatedly with numerous shells, and suffered heavy damage. She recrossed the boom that she had broken four hours earlier. Steering north-east across the bay of Algiers, she was joined by the *Zetland* who, with other Hunt class destroyers, was bombarding the troublesome Cape Matifou battery. *Zetland* eventually took her in tow, but her damage was such that she sank the next day in deteriorating weather. She bore a name made famous by an earlier *Broke* in World War 1; thus her gallant action seemed a fitting end.

Early in the morning of 8 November, RAF Hurricanes and Spitfires began taking off from Gibraltar with the aim of supporting the anti-submarine activities in the landing areas, at that time being provided by the Fleet Air Arm aircraft from the carriers. The biggest problem for the Gibraltar based aircraft was the provision of fuel, and it was therefore essential that the local airfield of Maison Blanche

and Blida should be captured at the earliest moment possible, since the land based fighters would not have enough fuel to return to Gibraltar.

Shortly after 10.00am Hurricanes of No 43 Squadron RAF landed at Maison Blanche, when it was known that the airfield was in American hands.

Fighter cover had till then been provided solely by Seafires and Martlets of the FAA flying from the fleet carriers *Victorious* (flag of Admiral Lyster) and *Formidable*, and the smaller carriers *Argus* and *Avenger*.

Sub Lieutenant R. B. Phillips was flying a Martlet in 888 Squadron, borne in the *Formidable*, and gives a first hand account of the naval aviation picture.

'The Torch operation, although not the first invasion in which we in 888 Squadron had taken part, was far and away the biggest and most important we had yet encountered. To our surprise and with mixed feelings we found ourselves operating with US insignia on our aircraft. Over the period of the operation, there was plenty of incident both self-induced and enemy-inspired, such as that on 7 November, when an Albacore of 820 squadron having just been repaired after a barrier incident, ditched alongside HMS *Milne* not five minutes prior to a Martlet of 893 Squadron performing likewise alongside another of the screen destroyers. During the evening, the dusk patrol of 888 Squadron landed on during an air-raid alert, dodging about amongst the ack-ack being fired in every direction by the Force.

'On 8 November, the day of the invasion, Martlets from 893 Squadron (Lieutenant (A) Pearson RN) and Seafires from 885 Squadron (Lieutenant R. H. Carver RN) were briefed to strafe Maison Blanche but this was abandoned due to weather although the Seafires shot down a Vichy Glen Martin en route. 888 Squadron (Captain F. D. G. Bird RM) provided air cover for the force from first light until dusk and, amazingly, no enemy activity was encountered.

'Next day, however, reconnaissance Ju88s from Cagliari took an interest in proceedings and one was shot down in flames by Martlets of 888 Squadron (Lieutenant (A) D. M. Jeram, RN, and S/Lt (A) W. Astin, RNVR), the crew baling out to be recovered by one of the escorting destroyers. The German crew in fact floated past the *Formidable* not more than 50 yards away to the accompaniment of very rude noises and gestures from the ship's company.

'Enemy air activity continued into the evening and the dusk patrol of 888 Squadron, disturbed no doubt by friendly ack-ack from the fleet, were diverted to the *Victorious* after one of their number had spread his aeroplane and remaining fuel across *Formidable*'s flight deck.

'Patrol activity continued over the ensuing days, enlivened by many hair-raising take-offs and landings, notably by the Martlets which on take-off had an insidious built-in tendency to weave hideously down the flight deck, leaving trails of white smoke from much-abused brake drums prior to lurching into the air somewhere over B Turret! The news that Martlets were landing-on or taking-off invariably, from all corners of the ship, brought out the Goofers, many of whom never saw the light of day except on such occasions, in gleeful anticipation of "something new again today"! They usually congregated on what came to be known as Goofers Bridge.'

While on the subject of naval aviation it is worth recording that owing to the delay in the installation of radio at Maison Blanche for communication with Gibraltar and the HQ ship *Bulolo*, a naval Walrus was flown to the airfield to serve as a temporary signal station and to provide early warning of approaching enemy aircraft.

On the whole the operations on land had gone well, and in most places there had been no opposition. It was mentioned above that when Fort Sidi Ferruch had been taken in the early hours, the Commander, General Mast, welcomed the commando troops. Upon formally surrendering the fort he offered transport to take the commando troops to the airfield at Blida, but warned that the French there might resist. Some of the troops in the neighbourhood were friendly, some were not, and a clash was possible with the arrival of the invading troops. The whole situation however was overtaken by an exceptional event, the surrender of the airfield without bloodshed to a naval pilot and his fighter patrol from HMS *Victorious*. But let Commander B. H. C. Nation relate his own story.

'The part of this rather strange wartime drama from the time I landed at Blida to the time I took off again and

Above: Plenty of transport was landed. This picture was taken at Algiers docks./*IWM*

Left: A French soldier making friends with British and American troops outside the hotel in Algiers where Italians were under guard./*IWM*

Above right: British paratroops after disembarking at Algiers./*IWM*

the reason which prompted the French General to surrender his military base so swiftly has never been told before in any detail.

'Soon after dawn on the morning of 8 November 1942, HMS *Victorious* flew off her Grumman Martlet fighters to carry out a patrol over the Vichy French airfield at Blida about 40 miles South West of Algiers. I was the leader of this fighter patrol and, as we climbed away heading for the North African coast, we saw, spread out below us, the

massive Allied invasion fleet approaching the beaches – it was a fantastic sight and one which I shall never forget.

'We crossed the coast and headed inland. Our orders were to prevent any aircraft from taking off and to report by R/T to the ship any information on troop movements.

'We encountered a small amount of anti-aircraft fire as we approached our target but the firing petered out after a few minutes. As we flew round the airfield we could see a large number of dispersed aircraft, anti-aircraft gunners manning, but not firing, their guns and farm workers in the surrounding fields waving their handkerchiefs. There seemed very little activity going on below us and even the aircraft ground crews were conspicuous by their absence. I therefore reported to the ship that I thought the French had given in and were ready to surrender. The ship's Air Staff found this difficult to believe and asked whether we were over the right airfield. Luckily I was able to report that the name 'Blida' was written in large white letters in the middle of the airfield. I then asked the ship if I could land and accept the surrender and a few minutes later I received a message from my Admiral that I could land "If I thought it was safe to do so". An enemy airfield may not, perhaps, be the most salubrious place to land on – never-

theless I felt it was the right thing to do and the element of surprise would certainly be in my favour.

'I told my pilots what I was going to do and asked them to cover my approach and landing and, if the French opened fire on me, they were to 'blitz' the airfield and leave me to my own devices to get away as best I could. In the event I landed without incident and taxied towards a group of officers, switched off my engine, climbed out of my aeroplane and drew my revolver. I ordered one of the officers to take me to his commanding officer – in the most appalling French – and with my revolver pointing at his back we marched to the administrative buildings. We passed a number of French soldiers with rifles but they made no attempt to stop me. Outside the main building two sentries with fixed bayonets came to attention as we walked in, which I thought at the time was a courteous gesture on their part until I realised that the salute was, of course, for their own officer.

'While all this was going on, the Martlets were flying low round the airfield in a very purposeful manner and I had no doubts at all that they would open up with their machine guns if the French tried to interfere with my aircraft in any way. This was a comforting thought as we entered the Commandant's office. An elderly General rose from his desk and was somewhat surprised to find himself looking down the barrel of a revolver. I told him that he had no alternative but to surrender his base immediately, otherwise a striking force from the carriers would be launched with instructions to bomb Blida until they gave in. He said he needed time to discuss this with his officers so I told him he could make one internal telephone call but, that if I was not in the air within 15 minutes, the ship

would be informed by the patrolling Martlets and his airfield would be bombed. He spoke for two or three minutes on the telephone and, as he was doing this, I heard the sound of distant gunfire which meant that the commando troops were closing in. I think this decided him for he picked up a piece of paper from his desk, and wrote that the base at Blida was at the disposal of the Allied Forces. Thus the airfield with some 60 aircraft and a garrison of 500 troops surrendered without a shot being fired.

'I had now been on the ground for nearly half an hour and was anxious to re-join my pilots in the air and return to the carrier so, using the same French Officer as a hostage in case of any last minute tricks, I walked back to my aeroplane, still keeping the unfortunate Frenchman covered.

'As I taxied away from him, I gave him a smile but I don't think he had much of a sense of humour as he gave me a very cold and hostile look – perhaps one can really hardly blame him!'

French resistance stiffened during the forenoon of 8 November, especially at the fortress of Cape Matifou on the eastern side of the Bay of Algiers, and also at the fortresses of Duperre and L'Empereur guarding the harbour. At one time it seemed that a battle might be imminent, but by the afternoon the obstinate fortresses had been silenced by the bombing from FAA Albacores and bombardment by the cruiser *Bermuda*.

But the wind freshened from the north-east, thus delaying the disembarkation of stores ashore and wrecking some 50 landing craft in the course of the day. During the afternoon enemy aircraft were seen shadowing, and at dusk both the *Sheffield* and the *Bermuda* were attacked repeatedly in a

Left: A troop ship docking at Algiers./*IWM*

Below: British paratroops marching away after disembarking at Algiers./*IWM*

Right: A Valentine tank being unloaded in the docks at Algiers./*IWM*

series of single torpedo attacks by aircraft. They only managed by the use of much helm at high speed to elude all torpedoes. Transports at the anchorages were also attacked, two being hit; and the Hunt class destroyer *Cowdray* was so badly damaged that she had to be beached eastward of Algiers harbour. Three German aircraft were destroyed.

In Algiers General Ryder had been conferring with General Juin who represented Admiral Darlan. A cease-fire was to be declared in Algiers and the neighbourhood, and Allied occupation was to take place at 7.0pm, the harbour batteries and all forts being taken over. Transports would move to anchorages in the Bay of Algiers. By nightfall the American 39th and 168th RCTs and the British 11th Brigade Group were ashore, but heavy swell and rising wind put a temporary stop to unloading at the beaches where the many casualties to landing craft had recurred. With Commodore J. A. V. Morse (Commodore Algiers

designate) in control of Algiers harbour, disembarkation would continue smoothly in the morning.

'At dawn the next day November 9th,' says the official report, 'the *Bulolo* entered harbour and berthed alongside, receiving an enthusiastic welcome from a large crowd of onlookers.' Actually it was a little more exciting than that. It was a day of increasing enemy air activity, directed particularly against the Allied ships in Algiers Bay. In an attack at 4.30pm there were some 30 Ju 88s and He 111s. Little damage was done and half a dozen aircraft were brought down. Commander P. M. B. Chavasse who as Staff Torpedo Officer on Burrough's staff was serving in the *Bulolo*, describes the scene, but makes no mention of his own brave act that day when, according to Commander T. C. Russell, the Staff Navigating Officer, 'Chavasse did a fine piece of work on an unexploded circling torpedo, which landed on shore.'

'At first light *Bulolo* was attacked by a single enemy

Left: Under watchful eye of an American soldier with a Tommy Gun, German prisoners are embarked at Algiers./*IWM*

Below left: Air raid at Algiers. Flat and shops which were damaged./*IWM*

was clear that she could not possibly stop in time and that she would drive into the sea wall. Admiral Burrough in no way interfered but, in the later moments, gave the order "everyone lie down". I found myself lying beside Commodore Morse, having a furious argument with him as to whether the mast would fall forward or aft. However, *Bulolo* came to a lurching stop, her bows driving into a thick bank of mud, and rising across the street to puncture the houses beyond.'

Another witness J. M. McConnell says of *Bulolo*, 'She was poised there for several seconds before sliding back and refloating. The assembled citizens of Algiers were most impressed with this magnificent feat of ship handling and modern berthing technique. Everyone else merely breathed a sigh of relief.'

Thus did the city of Algiers pass safely into Allied hands.

It is of interest to conclude this long chapter with a postscript from Mr Leslie Baldwin who was in the *Awatea* for the landing at Sidi Ferruch and who comments on that enigmatic character Darlan.

'I remember the lights of the place coming into view during the early hours and operations began to get under way. I did not myself go ashore until after daybreak when we had moved closer inshore.

'At Sidi Ferruch we occupied seaside villas amid a profusion of colourful flowers and one could not help noticing the contrast between this peaceful scene and the comings and goings of landing craft and the speedy erection of anti-aircraft guns on the beach. There was slight enemy air activity, but we spent the day unmolested, with frequent rumours of what was happening in Algiers itself, the chief of which was that Darlan had been arrested in the town. He was looked upon as an enemy at the time and there was some jubilation which later turned to surprise when it was known that a deal had been arranged with him. The following day we drove into Algiers by lorry, the first British naval personnel to enter the town. We had rifles at the ready but no cause to use them. On the contrary the populace had turned out in force and seemed overjoyed to see us.

Later that day there was rather more air activity, but by that time Spitfires had arrived and I have a vivid recollection of an enemy plane being pursued across Algiers Bay, exchanging fire all the way until it finally crashed into the bay. We knew then that the day was won. A postscript to this story may be of interest.

'We eventually found a temporary home in the local Lycee and I was interested to look through some of the exercise books left behind by the students. The success of the Petain anti-British propaganda was obvious. There was not a good word to be found for the British in any of them. Fortunately the adult population seemed to remember happier times and by them we were generally welcomed.'

aircraft' writes Chavasse, 'doubtless thinking us a soft target. When it was hit and brought down I remember Admiral Burrough throwing his hat in the air. That was the last he saw of it.'

Unknown to those in *Bulolo*, a near miss bomb had damaged engine-room telegraphs. Engine-room response therefore, to the call for full speed astern, would be anything but immediate.

'The arrival of *Bulolo* in Algiers was spectacular.' continues Chavasse, 'We were intended to berth, port side to, on the Railway Jetty. There was a sea wall ahead at the end of the jetty and, beyond that, a street with houses on the other side. A fairly strong wind blew from astern and we came in fast. A crowd of French on the jetty cheered us. When *Bulolo*'s engines were eventually put to full astern it

Assault on Oran

In much the same way as the slow and fast convoys for Algiers had, until dark on 7 November, appeared to be steaming for Malta, so did the two Oran assault convoys KMS(O)1 and KMF(O)1, having joined together at 4.0pm that day, at position CR, some 50 miles north-west of Oran. At that moment the CNTF under Commodore Thomas Troubridge with his broad pendant in the HQ ship *Largs*, comprised 34 transports and 70 warships, the latter force including the carrier *Furious*, the auxiliary carriers *Biter* and *Dasher*, and the cruisers *Jamaica*, *Aurora*, and *Delhi*, together with destroyers, sloops, corvettes trawlers, and minesweepers. In addition, the submarines P 54 and *Ursula* were to act as homing beacons off the Oran beaches. The battleship *Rodney* would, with three destroyers, join CNTF later. With Troubridge in the *Largs*, were Major-General Lloyd R. Fredendall of the US Army and Major-General James H. Doolittle of the US Army Air Force.

There were to be two assaults to the west of Oran in sectors X and Y, and one to the east in sector Z, with a supplementary landing on R beach in sector Z: see Map 4, page 39 . The SNOLs were Captain G. R. G. Allen for the X beaches; Captain E. V. Lees for the Y beaches; and Captain C. D. Graham for the Z beaches.

Having met at the rendezvous at 4.0pm, ships then formed into the various groups which had been detailed for the three assault areas. Sector Z was to be given the strongest force, so that the little port of Arzeu, 20 miles to the east of Oran, could be taken early in the operation.

The port of Oran lies only 245 miles east of Gibraltar as compared with the 427 miles which separate Gibraltar and Algiers. Nevertheless this was still too far for effectual use of Gibraltar's fighters, and recourse was, as at Algiers, to use the aircraft of the three carriers for fighter cover, and the *Furious*'s Albacores for attacks on French airfields.

The chosen landing beaches were at strategic places spread roughly over a distance of 50 miles of the coast, with Oran in the middle and the airfields of La Senia and Tafaraoui within reasonable approach. A column of Armoured Combat Command was to land in the X sector with orders to capture and isolate the small Lourmel airfield ten miles from the landing place. Y sector at Les Andalouses, only 15 miles west of Oran, was to be the landing place for the 26th Regimental Combat Team whose objective was the capture of Oran after gaining control of the heights lying to the west of Oran.

There were to be four landings in the Z sector 20 miles eastward of Oran, the objectives being the capture of Arzeu and the coastal defences there, (particularly Fort de la Pointe), the capture of Oran from the south, and the capture of the airfields at La Senia and Tafaraoui, distant some 20 miles and 25 miles respectively from the Z sector landing beaches.

Barely four miles westward from Oran was the naval base of Mers-el-Kebir, the scene of the British navy's attack on the French fleet on 3 July 1940, after France's capitulation to Germany, an attack which was the cause of the present expected bitter French opposition. Because of

the importance of capturing the port of Oran intact, so that follow-up convoys could be berthed at an early date, a frontal assault was to be made on Oran harbour by two ex-US coastguard cutters manned by the British and renamed *Walney* and *Hartland*. They were to fly the American flag as well as the White Ensign, and were to land two parties of American combat troops and anti-sabotage parties with orders to seize the shore batteries covering the harbour and to prevent scuttling of ships and immobilisation of harbour facilities.

The 104 ships of the fast and slow convoys, having met at rendezvous CR at 4.00pm on 7 November, and been sorted and formed into the requisite groups, combined together on their courses for Malta until dark. This was executed generally by the slow convoy opening out its columns to admit those of the fast convoy. The various assault groups (their assigned role in brackets) were as below; they were detached from the spurious track leading to Malta, at the following carefully pre-arranged times after dark in order to arrive at their respective release positions at the appropriate time. The details below will be more interesting and comprehensible if reference is made to Map 3.

At 6.00pm, Group VIII comprising escort and the LST *Bachaquero* (to land tanks at X beach) altered course southward for position CW, submarine P 54 acting as beacon; they were due to arrive at CW at 8.45pm.

At 6.00pm, the same time that Group VIII were altering course for position CW, Group IX altered course to the

south-east for position CE, five and a half miles off-shore, where the submarine *Ursula* was acting as homing beacon. Group IX comprised an escort and the two LSTs *Misoa* and *Tasajera* (to land tanks at Z).

At 6.15pm, Group I comprising an escort with the LSIs *Batory*, with SNOL (X) embarked, *Queen Emma, Prinses Beatrix*, and the transports *Benalbenach, Mary Slessor, Mark Twain* and *Walt Whitman*, (altogether to lower 39 landing craft at X beach), altered course for position CW; they were due to arrive there at 9.45pm.

At 6.15pm, Group II comprising an escort with the LSIs *Glengyle*, with SNOL (Y) embarked, *Monarch of Bermuda, Llangibby Castle, Clan Mactaggart*, and the transport *Salacia*, (to lower 45 landing craft at Y beach), altered course for position CW; they were due to arrive there at 9.45pm.

Of the above, Groups I and II were to part company on arrival at CW, Group I proceeding to X beach, while Group II, led by the cruiser *Aurora*, proceeded to Y beach.

Also at 6.15pm, Groups III and IV altered course to the south-east for position CE, being due there at 9.30pm, led by the cruiser *Jamaica*. Group III (destined for Z beach) comprised strong escort and LSIs *Durban Castle, Duchess of Bedford, Warwick Castle, Ettrick, Tegelberg, Reina del Pacifico* with SNOL (Z) embarked, and the LSG *Derwentdale*. Group IV (destined for R beach in the Z sector) comprised, with escort, the medium sized LSIs *Ulster Monarch, Royal Ulsterman*, and the *Royal Scotsman*. Groups III and IV, due

Above left: HMS *Boadicea* hit by French destroyer at Oran./*IWM*

Above: *Hartland* and *Walney* ramming the boom at Oran to land British and US troops./*From a painting by C. E. Turner*

Right: LSI *Glengyle* carrying troops, LCA and LCM./*A. Steer*

to arrive together at 11.15pm in the lowering position CZ for Z and R beaches respectively, carried between them 68 LCA, 14 LCM, and 3 LCS.

Following the above departures from the track for Malta there were still left on this route Groups V, VI, and VII. Group V consisting of ships whose role it was to land at Z beach after H hour but before daylight, altered course for position CE at 7.50pm, arriving there well after Groups III, IV, and IX, had passed through and moved to the release position at CZ. Groups VI and VII, consisting of ships that would not be required to transfer troops and equipment before daylight, left the Malta route 45 minutes after midnight to arrive at CZ after sunrise on 8 November.

Position CF, 25 miles north of Oran, was to be the rendezvous for the battleship *Rodney*, detached from Force H, to protect the anchorages from attack by enemy heavy forces. She, together with the carriers of the CNTF, the *Furious, Biter,* and *Dasher,* and the AA cruiser *Delhi*, were to rendezvous at CF at 5.30am on 8 November.

After leading in the Z beach and R beach groups, III and IV, *Jamaica* would be available to provide independent supporting fire off Z beach in the Gulf of Arzeu. The *Aurora* was to lead in Group II to the Y beach at Les Andalouses, and then patrol five miles north of Mers-el-Kebir, to destroy any French forces attempting to leave the harbour during darkness. During daylight she was to keep out of range of shore batteries.

In the X Sector

All appeared to be going according to plan. The weather was favourable and the sea was calm, but, as at Algiers, an unexpected set to the west was encountered. But even more unexpected was the appearance in X sector of a small French convoy of four ships steaming north-east, which straggled across the approach path of the assault convoy to X beach. The small convoy seemed to be even more surprised than the approaching transports and fled to the north-east, where they then sighted the assault convoy destined for the Y sector. This was too much. Understandably they turned tail, and later ran aground in a

position south and west of X beach. Their appearance however was not without effect, for it delayed the Allied minesweepers who then became overrun by the oncoming Allied transports.

As at Algiers, pilotage parties from submarines had examined the beaches prior to the landings, and folbots with a shaded light were to be stationed 400 yards off-shore. The flights of landing craft, after being lowered from the transports, were to be led by motor launches, with pilot officers embarked, to the folbots inshore, after which the craft would then push on ashore.

Nevertheless the assault generally got under way close to H hour 1.00am on 8 November. In the X sector the initial assault was delayed by no more than 35 minutes, when SNOL (X) in the *Batory*, ordered the minesweepers to get clear, and the landings to begin.

At X beach however, in spite of the various aids for finding Green beach and White beach the *Queen Emma*'s assault wave, which was the first to go in, failed to locate Green beach. The second wave, which was *Batory*'s had better luck and found Green beach successfully, only to discover that it was long, shallow, and exposed to the weather. Also the sand was soft ashore and this made it

Left: A light gun being lowered into landing craft off Oran./*IWM*

Below: US troops climbing down into landing craft off Oran./*IWM*

Below right: Landing craft with US troops about to proceed inshore./*IWM*

difficult to get the landed vehicles across the Green beach.

On the other hand White beach in this X sector was approached by the tank landing ship *Bachaquero*. Her captain, Lt-Cdr A. W. McMullen, RNR, carried out a quick survey between rocky headlands, and found the beach to be a 50 yard stretch in a well sheltered cove protected from the weather. White beach was therefore favoured and the others abandoned as soon as daylight revealed the situation in this somewhat isolated but important spot. Regrettably the extreme shallowness of the sea near the beach resulted in many of the heavy LCMs getting stuck in the sand so firmly that bulldozers had to be used to push them off. Of the 39 landing craft available in X sector, 13 were LCMs; only three of these LCMs remained serviceable, the others suffering damage to rudders and propellers. But no opposition was encountered here, and it appeared that Group I had taken the French completely by surprise. X sector's White beach, 30 miles from the nearest port, was to remain in use until 11 November, landing in all 3,242 men, 458 tanks and vehicles, and 1,170 tons of stores.

Lt-Cdr L. D. Redfarn, RNR, who was in the *Walt Whitman*, in charge of transport, writes: 'Our group was for X beach at Oran. We were due in at 1.00am and it was a dark night with a swell as from some distant storm. The shore navigation lights were on for the benefit of a French Coastal Convoy, which put back our arrival one hour. The 'lights' helped us to navigate our way in, for we could not see the blue stern light of the ship ahead, nor the minesweepers or the submarine which were there to guide us in. (I never did make the infra-red binoculars work).

'We anchored somewhere near the right spot, dropped our scrambling nets overside, then put the landing craft into the water. I think we were scheduled to clear our cargo in 36 hours. Whatever it was, we kept to schedule, in spite of a nasty swell that came up. I was on deck most of the time. There was always coffee in the percolator in the saloon, but I did have the request from the Chief Steward, "Would I come in on time when the hash hammer went, otherwise the stewards had to be paid overtime?". This, in the middle of the landing! There was as far as I know, no opposition on our beach. In fact the Arabs were soon helping to carry ammunition up the beach. There was some firing but it may well have come from trigger happy Americans announcing their arrival.

'There was an unexpected sand bar some distance out from the beach and larger landing craft had difficulty in off loading their cargo. When the landing was complete, the cargo ships were convoyed to Arzeu, on the other side of Oran.'

In the Y Sector

Meanwhile the ships of Group II, with the 26th Regimental Combat Team, had been led by the *Aurora* to the Y Sector release position, further east, and close to Les Andalouses. Here also the sea was calm, though with a growing swell, and the weather good. The first wave of LCAs from *Glengyle* and the *Monarch of Bermuda* were released at a quarter to midnight and proceeded inshore, led by a motor launch As soon as the infra-red light of the folbot beacon was sighted the motor launch withdrew for the second wave, and the landing craft continued inshore to land on Y's White beach. The craft from the *Monarch of Bermuda* lost touch with each other but arrived successfully, the first part at 1.00am on 8 November and the second part at

1.36am. *Glengyle*'s flotilla of 11 LCAs touched down at 1.16am; but an unexpected hindrance was discovered in the presence of a sand bar some 10 yards off shore on which the heavier landing craft such as the LCMs and LCPs grounded, causing great damage to rudders and propellers. The depth of water over the bar varied from six inches to three and a half feet. Inshore of the bar, the depth was as much as five feet.

A Sub-Lieutenant (now Lt-Cdr F. R. Jerram) in charge of one of the ten LCPs from the *Llangibby Castle*, writes: 'The

initial assault was made under cover of darkness. We had appalling supply problems; everything had to be ferried ashore, and ships had been incorrectly loaded, so that when ammunition was needed one had to hoist out innumerable quantities of other items to get at it. On the beach it had to be manhandled and we had great difficulties with the rising swell and a sand bar on which the LCPs grounded. I recall unloading a record player on to the beach on D day which indicated that priorities were not quite as one would expect.'

Left: US troops landing at Arzeu near Oran./*IWM*

Below left: American troops hopeful of non-resistance./*IWM*

Right: US troops at Arzeu fraternising with the natives./*IWM*

On the last subject, Lieutenant L. E. Craven, RNR, a navigator in the *Glengyle*, refers to the fact that the first items sent ashore in the LCM were the camp kitchens for the US Rangers.

Another Sub-Lieutenant (now Captain James Weir) also in charge of one of the *Llangibby Castle*'s LCPs comments on the difficulties of correct timing and the ordeal at the bar on each journey inshore.

'We were lowered at 11.45pm', he writes, 'and went off by divisions to the *Monarch*, who had not finished lowering when we arrived, so we had to wait about 10 minutes before going alongside'. All the ships were still slowly under way. 'Once there though, we still had to wait – one boat at each sally port, for another five minutes.

'The soldiers appeared to be heavily laden. ... We moved off by divisions towards *Glengyle* . . . and ran across the minesweeping trawlers sweeping the channel for the ships to enter the bay. Soon after this we reduced to a mere crawl to avoid overtaking LCA stragglers. We arrived on the beach, or more correctly on the bar, half an hour late.

'The soldiers floundered over the bar into thigh deep water and several fell over with the weight of their gear. I carried a platoon with two three-inch mortars, and some of the pieces were very heavy. Between the bar and the beach the water was mostly up to their chests.'

Soon after 3.00am a green light three star rocket shone out of the sky indicating success ashore, and the transports were then to go inshore and anchor. 'Now', continues Craven, 'I had to anchor five transports as close as possible to a semi-circular beach, very close together. We went in the dark, in line astern, close order, on a curving course, entirely on compass, echo sounder, and pitometer log. Not a bearing to be had at any time. Thank God I did not let the merchant navy down! At full light there was the whine of missiles from the heaven above, then a gunflash was seen over a mountain well inland and we knew that we were being bombarded. . . .'

In the Z Sector

The landings in the Z sector on four beaches in the vicinity of the small port of Arzeu, were on a much greater scale than those at X and Y, and involved 85 landing craft of which 68 were the troop-carrying LCAs. Led by the HQ ship *Largs* and the cruiser *Jamaica*, and accompanied by a strong escort of three destroyers, five corvettes, a sloop, a dozen minesweepers, four motor launches, and the anti-aircraft cruiser *Delhi*, Groups III and IV proceeded to the release position CZ.

Group III comprised ten large troop-carrying LSIs *Duchess of Bedford*, *Warwick Castle*, *Ettrick*, *Tegelberg*, *Reina del Pacifico* (carrying the SNOL for Z sector, Captain Q. D. Graham), and the large LSG *Derwentdale* carrying

14 LCM for the Army vehicles. Group IV comprised the smaller LSIs *Royal Scotsman*, *Royal Ulsterman*, and *Ulster Monarch*.

The requirement was to land 29,000 officers and men, 2,400 vehicles, and 14,000 tons of stores, and it was fortunate that the landings were entirely unopposed, at this strategic area which surrounded the port of Arzeu. The beaches extended for several miles, the sand was firm, the gradient easy, and the exits were accessible. All seemed well, if the weather remained suitable. But there was plenty of time for the French to recover from initial surprise, and the potential hazards were numerous.

Frontal Assault on Oran Harbour

Although the landings along the Oran beaches had been so successful, the direct frontal assault by the two ex-American coastguard cutters the *Walney* and the *Hartland* proved disastrous. The attack had the same objective as at Algiers, the purpose being the capture of key points and the prevention of sabotage. It was initially due to take place at H hour but at the discretion of Commodore Troubridge, the Task Force Commander, could be delayed up to two hours, after which it could be cancelled if the French were found to be alert and resisting the beach landings, or alternatively if the French proved friendly. By 3.00am, when Troubridge decided to execute the plan, the French were very much on the alert and were soon to show every hostility in the harbour and elsewhere. There was no inclination on their part to observe the frequently and loudly broadcast phrase, '*Ne tirer pas: nous sommes vos amis*'.

The Commanding Officer of the *Hartland*, Lt-Cdr G. P. Billot, RNR, writes: 'We were sent in to Gibraltar to embark American combat troops by night and on the evening of 7 November detached with orders to enter Oran Harbour and capture key objectives. While breaking the boom we were caught by searchlights and heavy fire from machine guns and batteries which soon immobilised both ships which eventually sank with heavy casualties. The survivors were all taken prisoner by the French.' Being severely wounded himself, and temporarily blinded by a splinter Billot was taken to hospital. The Commanding Officer of the *Walney*, Lt-Cdr P. C. Meyrick, was among those wiped out in the point blank broadsides from a French destroyer. In both ships there was indescribable carnage below on the mess decks among the parties of troops waiting to land. One of those on deck who miraculously survived, was Capt F. T. Peters, RN, in command of the expedition, who by an ironical turn of fate perished a few days later when flying home after being released by the French. He was posthumously awarded the Victoria Cross and the American Distinguished Service Cross.

There were few survivors, and in view of accusations of brutality to prisoners it is important to quote an extract relevant to this point as in the second of the letters below.

G. Smith of the *Walney* writes: 'We were rather concerned at the order for the Stars and Stripes to be flown on the mainmast above the White Ensign. . . . I was the only survivor from the Communications Branch, and was informed that from the total crew of over 200, only just over 40 survived.'

R. M. Pocock, a coder in *Hartland*, writes: 'Caught in an all-exposing searchlight tattoo, hit many times, we waddled towards the berth that was to be the graveyard of the ship and many of her crew and passengers.

'I was in the Wireless Room, on the upper deck, and the room was hit by a shell and the seven occupants wounded: some mortally. . . . We were eventually taken and put in a cell-like structure. At daybreak interrogation commenced and iodine poured on wounds as rudimentary first aid. At about this time the base was shelled by the *Rodney*. . . .

'It was an experience to be marched in plimsolls, under-pants, and vests, some miles through a town where the residents vented their spleen by spitting and throwing stones.'

After further comment concerning painful treatment in hospital at a time when there was a growing shortage of medical assistance, Pocock concludes: 'There still remains the overriding memory that the abortive attempt to capture a well armed naval port in that way was due to a gross error of judgement at High Command. The courage of the Americans in the face of their first involvement in the European war was such that Hollywood films fade into insignificance.'

Follow-Up

The failure of the frontal assault with the loss of the two ships and heavy casualties, was in itself sufficiently tragic, but it also allowed French ships to escape under cover of darkness and permitted the French to sabotage docks and berthing facilities in the harbour. In the meantime the British warships on patrol had not been idle. At 5.27am before first light on 8 November the *Aurora* opened fire on the searchlight illuminating the *Hartland*; and shortly afterwards engaged, at a range of three miles, a French destroyer attempting to leave harbour, which she sank. By first light, the channels to the inner anchorage in Z sector had been swept to allow the large transports to move inshore. Also by first light the American Rangers had taken two batteries at Arzeu. A 75mm field gun nevertheless managed to score three hits on the *Reina del Pacifico* though without causing casualties. At 6.00am, two French destroyers left Oran, presumably to attack transports, and were engaged by the British destroyers *Calpe* and

Bottom left: A destroyer lays a smoke screen round a transport off Oran./*IWM*

Right: US assault ship *Thomas Stone,* the only casualty prior to the assault, safely at Algiers./*IWM*

Boadicea and the cruiser *Aurora*. The *Boadicea* was hit forward, but one of the Frenchmen was driven ashore and the other returned to harbour. Also the French chasseur *La Surprise* was engaged and sunk by the British destroyer *Brilliant*. The *Brilliant* herself suffered little damage, but her captain and four others were killed by shell splinters. She picked up French survivors and then returned to the anchorage.

In the Y sector, off Les Andalouses, ships were receiving the unwelcome attentions of the 7.6 inch gun battery at Jebel Santon, 1,060 feet above Mers-el-Kebir, nine miles to the eastward. Despite this, 4,330 men and 77 vehicles had landed by 7.00am, and by 8.00am tanks were being brought ashore. Jebel Santon again opened fire on the Y sector transports just before 9.00am, and continued to be a distinct threat to the landing ships in spite of the fire from the British warships on patrol.

Captain R. A. H. Arnold, RA, was a forward observation officer attached to the American 16th RCT landing at Arzeu for the purpose of calling for and observing bombardment support. 'The bombardment fleet', he writes, 'included *Rodney, Jamaica* and five destroyers, and I personally brought the fire of the *Jamaica* and the *Farndale* against what little resistance there was on the east flank.'

The batteries du Santon and Pointe Canastel on either side of and close to Oran were however of sterner stuff. The former scored a direct hit on the *Llangibby Castle* at 9.17am and on the *Monarch of Bermuda* at 11.00am, thus forcing the transports to shift berth further west in the hope of being out of range, and this caused a regrettable reduction in the speed of unloading.

Bearing in mind Admiral Mahan's edict that 'Ships are unequally matched against forts', it is instructive to read extracts from an account of the bombardment of Santon, by Lt-Cdr J. G. Forbes (now Cdr) who was the navigating officer of the battleship *Rodney*.

'At 9.00am *Aurora* called for fire from *Rodney* and six minutes later we opened up with our 16in guns and fired sixteen rounds without any reply from the shore battery. Soon after 3.00pm we began firing again but there was still

no reply from the fort and the rest of the day passed without incident.

'During this operation, *Rodney* was steaming up and down between Oran and Mers-el-Kebir and we were doing our best to keep the target within range of the main armament but outside the maximum range of the shore batteries (reputed to be 21,000 yards), and at the same time taking what precautions we could against possible U-boat attack.

'Calculating the range before opening fire was a matter of some difficulty. The Gunnery Officer had constructed a special bombardment chart but the only means of fixing the ship was by cross bearings of rather indistinct objects on the shore. It was, therefore, a great relief to the Navigating Officer when the first round landed near the target! Spotting was done initially by the ship's own Walrus aircraft, but unfortunately she was damaged by antiaircraft fire on the first day and, although the crew escaped unhurt, she had to be sunk.

'The next morning, 9 November, *Rodney* was still patrolling up and down waiting for instructions when, at 8.30am, Fort Santon opened fire on us. Although the range was 22,000 yards, say 11 miles, some shells fell only just short on the ship's starboard quarter. This brought the Surgeon-Commander (never an early riser) rushing out of his cabin to find out what was disturbing him!

'On 10 November we received an urgent demand for fire on Santon which was firing HE shell at the approaching US troops. The range of Santon was 17 miles, the visibility was poor, and the land near the fort entirely obscured by cloud. As the US troops were only 600 yards from the target, the first round was fired with a margin of safety, but the great majority of all subsequent rounds fell within a hundred yards of the battery. Shortly afterwards, Fort Santon capitulated.'

With the capitulation on 10 November of Santon, which had resisted so strongly, the end was near. It is evident, however, that resistance meanwhile had been widespread. Let us return to D-day, 8 November, when the landing forces were making steady progress towards Tafaraoui airfield all the morning and captured it soon after midday. Early in the forenoon of that day Albacores from the *Furious*, escorted by her own Seafires and the Sea Hurricanes from the *Biter* and *Dasher*, effectively attacked the airfields at La Senia and Tafaraoui, and for the loss of one Albacore and one Sea Hurricane destroyed 70 aircraft on the ground, all of which were later found to have been fully armed and fuelled and ready to attack at short notice. Unfortunately, the paratroopers flown out from England to seize the airfields, met bad weather over Spain, became scattered and failed in their mission. Early in the afternoon of the 8th, after Tafaraoui had been captured by combat troops, 26 American Spitfires from Gibraltar touched down at Tafaraoui. La Senia, however, less than five miles from Oran, withstood the siege of the 1st US Infantry Division who were advancing from the south and from the east, until the evening of the 9th. With the fall of La Senia, captured with 500 prisoners and 90 aircraft by the Armoured Combat Command the way was made clear for the final assault on the morning of the 10th.

Increasingly strong resistance had been met by the 16th and 18th RCTs on D-day as they advanced from Arzeu towards Oran, making good a distance of up to 15 miles on that day. Meanwhile the 26th RCT moved steadily eastwards from the Y sector towards the vicinity of Oran overcoming all opposition and capturing Aine-el-Turk on the way.

At the beaches there was increasing congestion and work was hampered by a growing swell and the stranding of a number of LCMs. This became so bad at the Z sector, that ships were transferred to Arzeu Harbour. By the 9th swell had increased so much in Y sector that unloading operations were suspended, though only temporarily, and the Allies continued to build up ashore and gain ground, while encountering French infantry and tanks. At one

stage supporting fire was provided by the Hunt class destroyer *Farndale*, as advised by Arnold the FOO attached to the 16th RCT, and described above.

Fighting continued all through D + 1, 9 November. At sea on that day, anti-submarine patrols continued with a force of three destroyers, two sloops, eight sweepers and four corvettes off Arzeu, and the *Rodney*, bombarded Fort du Santon several times before withdrawing after dark to patrol 30 miles off Oran. Santon continued to resist strongly as already described by Lt-Cdr Forbes. The *Aurora* repeated her successful patrol of the previous day, D-day, and with the *Jamaica*, engaged Vichy destroyers, driving one ashore in flames and forcing the other to retire.

The morning of 10 November was fine and clear. The *Llangibby Castle* and the *Monarch of Bermuda* having completed unloading at Y sector beaches both proceeded at daylight independently for Gibraltar. For the remainder, unloading continued, though much hampered by sand bar and the various bottlenecks that had developed. On this morning the 1st US Infantry Division and the Armoured Combat Command B had closed in for the final assault on the city of Oran. Their co-ordinated attack, launched at 7.37am, met stiff opposition, but by 11.00am they had entered the city, and Commodore Troubridge was able to make the following signal to NCFX at Gibraltar:

'Army in Oran appears to be capitulating. Sign that French Navy also give up.'

Capitulation was announced at noon on 10 November. At 12.30pm the French formally surrendered to General Fredendall. Thus did the city of Oran pass into Allied hands 59 hours after the initial landing.

Below: *Hartland* blows up after charging the boom at Oran./*H. B. Hamilton*

America Invades French Morocco

Particulars of the forces planned for the American assault on Casablanca, under Maj-Gen Patton, were given in Chapter Five. It will be recalled that Admiral Hewitt was to b[e] [i]n command of the Western Naval Task Force. Unlike th[e] [E]NTF and the CNTF whose assault convoys and warsh[ip]s had formed into the requisite groups only after entry into the Mediterranean, the WNTF left American waters as an entity, the rendezvous for all forces being eastward of Bermuda on 28 October, after the aircraft carrier group had sortied from that island.

The Force arrived in the vicinity of the coast of northwest Africa early on 7 November. Hewitt had to make a difficult decision on receipt of a forecast that on D-day, 8 November the 'surf would be 15 feet high and landings impossible'. On being advised by his meterological officer, however, that the weather would be moderating locally, he decided to go ahead with the landings as planned. Though risky, this was preferable to chances which would attend postponement or the alternative plan of entering the Mediterranean where there could well be heavy enemy submarine concentrations. Psychologically there was also much to be said for avoiding delay. It was a bold decision which in the event was thoroughly justified.

By [?].ooam on 7 November the weather was fine, the north[-]easterly wind was moderating, and the rough sea was easing[.] At this time, in accordance with the plans, the Southern Attack Group, under Rear-Adm Davidson, altered course to the south, leaving both the Northern Attack Group and the Centre Attack Group to continue their tracks eastward. See Map 5.

Southern Attack Group Assault on Safi

In command of the 47th RCT and two battalions of tanks, was Maj-Gen E. N. Harmon. The primary object of the attack was to secure the port of Safi for the unloading of the General Sherman tanks which were being carried in the ex-train ferry *Lakehurst*. The tanks were to be regarded as a reinforcement if necessary for the Centre Attack Group's assault on Casablanca 110 miles further north.

The plan of the assault incorporated, as at Algiers and Oran, the employment of two old destroyers, the *Bernadou* and the *Cole* in a frontal attack. This was to be co-ordinated with the landing of troops simultaneously on the beaches, from where the attackers would assail the town of Safi from all directions. H hour was to be at 4.00am on 8 November.

The approach was made without incident, but the attack opened at 4.39am after a delay of 39 minutes caused by errors of identification and difficulty in locating the beacon submarine.

On entering the harbour the *Bernadou*, carrying an assault company specially trained in night operations, was fired upon by the 75mm guns of a shore battery and nearby machine guns. She replied immediately, but by the time *Bernadou* and *Cole* had gained the inner harbour, two heavy batteries of 130mm (5.5 inch) naval guns had opened fire.

It was now that the ships of the Fire Support Group came into action: these were the cruiser *Philadelphia* (flying Davidson's flag), the battleship *New York*, and the destroyer *Mervine*. This diverted the fire from the assault destroyers who were then able to land their troops to secure harbour installations and cut off the French in their barracks. All this was in darkness, and after a while firing ceased. With sunrise the firing was resumed, but by this time American aircraft were over the French batteries, spotting for the *New York* and *Philadelphia*. One battery was silenced soon after 7.00am, and a second at 9.30am.

Although there was no opposition at the beaches, various misfortunes attended the landings. In one case a beach was found to be enclosed by very high cliffs. Another beach proved too soft until a wire mesh was put down. At 5.30am the *Dorothea Dix* was hoisting out a truck carrying ammunition which burst into flames, lighting up the whole area before it exploded. Confusion then followed when it was thought by the *Knight* that a torpedo must have caused the bang. A few landing craft were set on fire. It was 9.25am before the first wave of troops landed: these were from the *Dorothea Dix*. It was encouraging to find that there was no opposition to the landings although there had been fierce fire initially from the naval batteries.

Despite the various misfortunes and resulting confusion Safi was securely in American hands by 2.30pm on 8 November, and the transports *Harris, Dix, Lyon*, and *Calvert* moving to an anchorage close to Safi harbour entrance from which the discharge of cargo could continue without serious disruption. The *Lakehurst* docked in the harbour soon after 3.00pm and was able to begin unloading her tanks.

Good weather, darkness, and the prompt and accurate fire support were quoted as the beneficial factors which allowed the Southern Attack Group to capture Safi with the loss of only nine landing craft and 10 soldiers. Air cover was available from the escort carrier *Santee* which was operating 40 miles off-shore; but because of dense fog which developed on the 9th, when a warning of an impending raid by 40 French aircraft was received, no attack developed. *Santee*'s bomber fighters however destroyed 20 grounded aircraft at Marrakesh 80 miles south-east of Safi.

By 10 November Harmon's force, supported from sea and air by Davidson's Attack Group was moving north-ward to Mazagan, which lies on the coast between Safi and Casablanca. Mazagan and a neighbouring bridge were in American hands by 11 November. See Map 5.

The Southern Attack Group's assault on Safi may therefore be regarded as highly successful.

Northern Attack Group Assault at Mehdia for Port Lyautey

At 3.00pm 7 November, eight hours after the Southern Attack Group had been detached, the remainder of the Western Naval Task Force divided into two groups, the Northern Attack Group continuing eastward towards Mehdia near Port Lyautey, the Centre Attack Group altering to a south-easterly course for Fedala near Casablanca. Their respective destinations were each about 75 miles distant ahead.

The Northern Attack Group was under the command of Rear-Admiral Munroe Kelly and the objective was to capture both the port of Port Lyautey and the airfield which lies close to it. The port was valuable strategically as it possessed a railway and had quays equipped with five ton cranes. It lies eight miles up the winding Wadi Sebou near the mouth of which is the small town of Mehdia; the latter was believed to be a useful landmark from seaward in an otherwise bare prospect of sandy hills. There were 9,000 men of the 9th RCT and the 2nd Armoured Combat Team, with attached units, all under Brigadier-General Truscott. Naval fire support from the battleship *Texas* (flag of R-Adm Kelly) and the cruiser *Savannah* was to be provided for the destruction of shore batteries and search-lights and as a cover against hostile ships, while the escort carrier *Chenango* provided air cover against both submarine and aircraft attack. Simultaneous landings of troops and equipment were to be made at five beaches on a stretch covering 10 miles of coastline with Mehdia approximately in the middle.

On arrival off the coast, a detached destroyer sent ahead by Kelly, failed to find the beacon submarine, and resort had to be made to a radar fix of the river entrance, which led to considerable delay in the transports arriving at their scheduled positions off Mehdia. This was at 11.30pm 7 November. H hour planned for the landings was 4.00am 8 November. It was intended that the first disembarked assault waves should be led inshore to the landing beaches by the three control vessels, *Osprey, Eberle*, and *Raven*, who were to rendezvous with the front line transports upon their arrival at strategic positions about 2½ miles off-shore from the various beaches: see Map 6.

The American flagship the 10,000-ton cruiser *Wichita.*/IWM

Though the sea was smooth there was a heavy swell. Disembarkation took much longer than anticipated, so that the first waves landed up to an hour and a half behind schedule. It was unfortunate also that about this time, 5.30am, a French Coastal Convoy of five lighted steamers blundered into the transport area, and warned the Kasba 5.5-inch naval battery at the mouth of the river of the presence of American ships. The element of surprise had by now been lost and the situation was not eased by the repeated broadcasting of a message from President Roosevelt. There had been no resistance by the French while darkness had lasted. And the only material setback to the landings had come from the Americans themselves, through the gunfire of the *Savannah* and those American destroyers who were attempting to destroy the Kasba battery before it could fire on the transports. The troops thus receiving the gunfire were the very ones who had been ordered by General Truscott to take the Kasba by assault. The plan had been that the Kasba must be captured immed-iately the troops were ashore. So far, much of the plan seemed to have misfired. Truscott later reported that the landings had turned into a 'hit or miss affair which would have spelled disaster against a determined enemy'.*

At dawn on 8 November the fourth and fifth assault waves were attacked on the beaches by aircraft as well as by shore batteries. Repeated efforts to silence batteries by support gunfire produced temporary alleviation. The Kasba battery nevertheless was able to force the transports to withdraw out of range to a position 15 miles off shore, and this seriously delayed the whole landing programme. Those battalions already ashore were greatly handicapped by lack of supplies, field artillery, and even the rubber boats required for those who were to cross the river to capture the Port Lyautey airfield.

*Morison *Two Ocean War*, p. 230

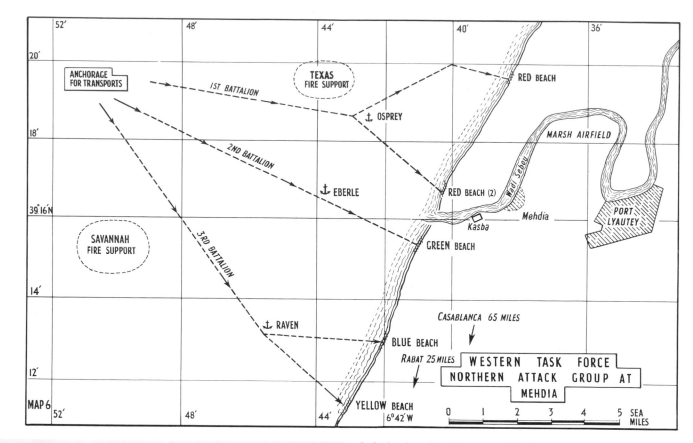

MAP 6

WESTERN TASK FORCE
NORTHERN ATTACK GROUP AT
MEHDIA

Left: An American destroyer, USS *Dallas* being watched by British sailors from a passing ship as it steams into port./*IWM*

Above right: Photograph of the 32,000-ton warship *Texas* at anchor./*IWM*

A false report at 11.00am 8 November that the Kasba fort had been taken, led to the old destroyer *Dallas* being ordered to proceed up river. Her entry was soon opposed however by accurate fire from the strongly resisting Kasba. Stubborn fighting continued, and by the end of the day the issue still hung in the balance. A further adverse factor arose for the invaders with the increasing surf on the beaches, and the congested exits where jeeps, trucks, light tanks, and stores were piling up fast.

Daybreak on the 9th brought no relief from the increasing swell, and the surf ran so high that landing operations were halted. Yet there was a growing demand for

tanks, ammunition, water, and medical supplies. In a desperate attempt to remedy this, unloading operations were resumed; many of the landing craft were swamped or stranded. But that night, the 1st Battalion seized high ground overlooking the Port Lyautey airfield, and the 3rd Battalion moved in to cross the river at daylight, the French wisely giving ground. The *Dallas* also headed once more up river. At daybreak on the 10th she came under heavy fire from an unidentified source, as she forced a passage through the entrance and proceeded upstream with her raider detachment of 75 men. Her arrival was hailed heartily by the 3rd Battalion who were crossing the river in what few rubber boats were available. It was at 7.37am that the *Dallas* arrived off Port Lyautey and under fire landed her troops who immediately attacked the airfield. This was captured, and by 11.00am on the 10th the first American aircraft had landed there.

During that morning the occupants of the fort at Kasba had put up a fierce resistance in reply to an attack by the 2nd Battalion. Air Support had then been called from the American carrier *Sangamon* whose aircraft at 7.00am laid on such an accurate bombing attack that the fort surrendered. The way was now clear for the transports, hitherto kept at bay by the Kasba battery, to come close inshore. Nevertheless a submarine scare caused them to proceed to sea for almost four hours before the inner anchorage was once

again declared reasonably safe. Unloading restarted with vigour at 2.24pm only 3,000 yards off the river entrance.

Neither the battleship *Texas* nor the cruiser *Savannah* had been effectual in silencing the Kasba battery, presumably because of the great risk of wiping out American troops in the vicinity and a failure to establish good communications with them. But both the *Savannah* and the *Texas* played an effective part in knocking out French tanks and infantry columns reported by spotting aircraft as coming from Rabat 25 miles to the south.

A novel form of attack on the approaching French troops was provided when an aircraft from the *Texas* dropped depth charges and achieved the destruction of three tanks. Dive bombers also took up the attack and the columns retreated towards Rabat.

The battle at Port Lyautey was brought to a conclusion very early on 11 November when the French defenders received orders on Admiral Darlan's authority, to cease resistance immediately: an appropriate event for Armistice Day. Shortly afterwards the Stars and Stripes flew Triumphantly over Port Lyautey.

Centre Attack Group Assault at Fedala for Casablanca

This was by far the strongest and most important assault, and was fraught with potential danger.

The main objective of the Centre Attack Group was the capture of Casablanca. Preparatory to this there were three direct tasks:

(i) to land troops and establish a five mile beachhead east of the small port of Fedala;

(ii) to capture the airfield three miles south-south-east of Fedala;

(iii) to silence the batteries at Cape Fedala if they should open fire.

Naval fire support was to be provided, as at the other simultaneous assaults, for the purpose of destroying searchlights, batteries, and French ships that might threaten the transports and the landings.

Cape Fedala lies 15 miles north-eastward along the coast from Casablanca. It has a small harbour at the south-west end of Fedala Bay which stretches for 2½ miles to the eastward.

The importance of Casablanca as the subject of eventual occupation by the Americans, lay not only in the acquisition of a large harbour, but also in the fact that the heads of French naval and military forces in Morocco had their posts there. In the event, through one misfortune after another, the successful achievement of the goal remained long in doubt, and the French continued to put up a respectable if pointless defence, aided not only by local troops and aircraft and shore batteries, but by their naval ships. Lying at Casablanca was the battleship *Jean Bart*, immobile but armed with four 15-inch guns which were fully operational. There was also the 6-inch cruiser *Primauguet*, destroyers, escort vessels, and nine submarines. The capture of Fedala was to be the toughest of the individual assaults by the three American Attack Groups on the Morocco coast, and it should be realised that failure there could have placed the whole Morocco operation in jeopardy. Moreover, the attacks on Safi and Port Lyautey,

miles north of the beaches, and included the hoisting out of the four scout boats that were to mark the four principal beaches. (See Map 7, page 97.) Unfortunately the second, third, and fourth divisions of transports which should have been in line abreast as was the first division, straggled badly, entirely upsetting the timing of the landing craft deployment plan. This mishap caused a slowing down of the disembarkation from the transports, with the result that only 18 out of 42 landing craft were available to proceed with the four piloting destroyers, *Wilkes, Swanson, Ludlow,* and *Murphy,* at H hour, 4.00am on 8 November, as scheduled, towards the landing craft line of departure. The latter was 3,500 yards from the beaches. The destroyers, followed by the slender first wave of landing craft, reached the line of departure at 4.45am, and the first wave of landing craft were then left by the destroyers to make their way inshore where the first landing began soon after 5.00am; over an hour behind schedule.

The night was fine with a gentle breeze and a calm sea, and there was a light at Cape Fedala which was helpful. Nor was there any opposition. However, a heavy surf was running on the beaches, and there was a falling tide which augmented its adverse effect. Nearly half the assault craft were wrecked during the opening stages of the attack. The second wave suffered even more so.

Furthermore, the westernmost scout boat beacon happened to be out of position so that the first four waves from the transport *Leonard Wood,* landing between 5.20am and 5.40am, ran on to the rocks. Out of 32 landing craft 21 were wrecked. Many of the troops carried in the wrecked craft were so heavily burdened with equipment that they were unable to regain their feet and were drowned in the surf.

But despite these tragic mishaps and difficulties 3,500 troops were landed in the first hour. Soon after 6.00am on 8 November it was light enough for the shore batteries to open up. Fire was returned by the pilot destroyers, supported by the cruisers *Augusta* and *Brooklyn*. By 7.30am,

executed at the same time would not greatly affect the issue one way or the other, if the Fedala venture failed.

The 2½ mile stretch of Fedala Bay where the beach landings were to take place was strongly defended at both ends. At the western end was the Port battery of 4-inch guns, and nearby, at Cape Fedala, though smaller, an almost inaccessible battery. At the eastern end of the bay at Pont Blondin was a battery of 5.5-inch guns. As a covering force the Americans had, under the command of Rear-Admiral Robert Giffen, the 35,000 ton battleship *Massachusetts* armed with nine 16-inch guns and twenty 5-inch, and the two 8-inch cruisers *Wichita* and *Tuscaloosa*. Also in attendance was the Fire Support Group for the Centre Attack, comprising the 10-inch heavy cruiser *Augusta* (flying Admiral Hewitt's flag) and the 6-inch cruiser *Brooklyn*, with the four destroyers *Wilkes, Swanson, Ludlow,* and *Murphy*.

In accordance with the plan, the first division of transports, four of them in line abreast, reached the lowering zone at midnight on 7 November. The work of lowering the landing craft was immediately begun in this area five

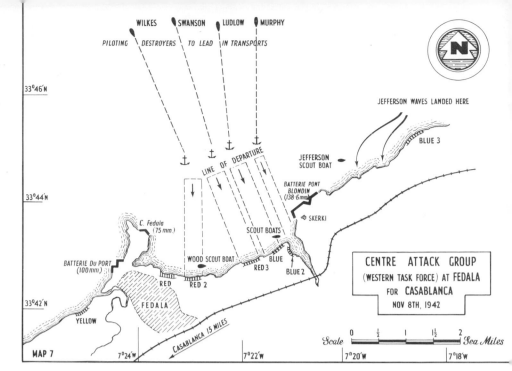

Below left: USS *Massachusetts* at 35,000 tons armed with nine 16-inch guns./IWM

Below: The accompanying cruiser USS *Philadelphia*./IWM

Map labels:

WILKES SWANSON LUDLOW MURPHY

PILOTING DESTROYERS TO LEAD IN TRANSPORTS

33°46′N

JEFFERSON WAVES LANDED HERE

BLUE 3

LINE OF DEPARTURE

JEFFERSON SCOUT BOAT

33°44′N

BATTERIE PONT BLONDIN (138·6mm)

SKERKI

C. Fedala (75 mm.)

SCOUT BOATS

BATTERIE DU PORT (100mm)

WOOD SCOUT BOAT

BLUE

RED 3

BLUE 2

33°42′N

RED

RED 2

FEDALA

YELLOW

CASABLANCA 15 MILES

MAP 7

7°24′W 7°22′W 7°20′W 7°18′W

CENTRE ATTACK GROUP (WESTERN TASK FORCE) AT FEDALA FOR CASABLANCA NOV 8TH, 1942

Scale 0 ½ 1 1½ 2 Sea Miles

all four of the 5.5-inch guns of the Pont Blondin battery had been silenced. The *Ludlow* and *Murphy* were both hit during this action but little damage was received.

Soon after 8.00am, French aircraft and the Fedala batteries began an attack on the landing craft and the troops on the beaches. As the batteries enfiladed the beaches and the approaches, it was essential to deal with them first, and the support destroyers returned the fire. But at 8.25am the destroyers came under fire from French ships that had emerged from Casablanca, and also a long range battery. Visibility was restricted by haze and smoke. As shells were falling close, the destroyers *Wilkes* and *Swanson* were compelled to withdraw northwards to join the *Augusta* and *Brooklyn* who opened fire at 8.43am on the French ships at a range of 6½ miles. This skirmish known as the first phase of the Naval Battle for Casablanca lasted for 21 minutes, and ended at 9.04am on 8 November soon after the French ships had turned back towards Casablanca, opening the range to 12 miles.

In the meantime the destroyer *Ludlow* had returned to the north-westward and having been the recipient of most of

the fire from the French ships had suffered crippling damage.

The lull in the action was short lived, for at 10.00am the French ships reappeared, this time reinforced by the cruiser *Primauguet*, all standing towards Fedala. The *Brooklyn* opened fire, being shortly followed at 10.27am by the *Augusta*, who fired 42 salvos at ranges up to 10½ miles. By 11.00am this second phase of the battle was practically over, the *Primauguet* having been withdrawn, badly damaged, to the refuge of Casablanca, and six out of seven of the French destroyers being sunk or completely disabled. They had all put up a stout and determined fight under cover of a thick smoke screen.

Meanwhile, from early daylight, aircraft from the 14,500 ton aircraft carrier *Ranger* had been very active. Her Wildcats had destroyed grounded planes in neighbouring airfields, and her dive bombers had attacked important targets in Casablanca harbour, and both had taken part in the naval action. Air cover and anti-submarine patrol had been provided by the fighters of the Air Group's auxiliary carrier *Suwanee*.

Right: US landing craft off Fedala,
November 1942./*USNI*

The naval battles seriously incommoded the movements of General Patton who was thereby confined in the *Augusta*. In fact it was to be two days before he eventually disembarked. And unfortunately, when he did, communication between US Army and Navy HQ virtually ceased, since the Army omitted to take with them a joint code for high grade messages. *Augusta* was thereby precluded from passing on to Army HQ ashore, any secret message she received from Allied Forces HQ at Gibraltar.

At noon on 8 November the French army at Fedala asked for armistice negotiations, but these were refused by Admiral Michelier who was Commanding French naval forces at Casablanca, despite the arrival on the scene of the American Covering Group under Rear-Admiral Giffen in the 16-inch battleship *Masachusetts*. Admiral Hewitt in the *Augusta* then ordered the destruction by air attack of all French naval ships emerging from Casablanca. Having already lost several ships and three submarines in harbour at Casablanca, with the *Jean Bart* and the *Primauguet* damaged, and the heavy batteries severely bombed, the French had already received considerable punishment. All that day, 8 November, the landings on the beaches continued, though seriously delayed and hampered by the fact that more than half of the landing craft had been lost. Bridges were taken in the town; and the high ground commanding Fedala and the beaches was occupied. At 2.30pm Fedala surrendered. By nightfall 7,750 troops had been put ashore on the beaches and Fedala harbour was under the control of the Americans. The French had not fared well in the air, having lost 55 aircraft. Opposition from Casablanca continued however. The heavy battery there at El Hank was still intact, having scored a hit earlier that day on the American cruiser *Wichita* of the Covering Group, which had wounded 14 men. And the 15-inch guns of the *Jean Bart* were again ready for action.

The next morning 9 November brought the first air attack on the transports and also an air attack on the *Brooklyn*. Unloading continued despite the heavy swell. The transports moved closer inshore, and by the evening some unloading was getting under way inside Fedala breakwater. Meanwhile American troops were advancing on Casablanca.

On 10 November two French ships attacked American troops on the beach near Casablanca, late in the forenoon. They themselves were then engaged at a range of nine miles by the *Augusta*. At 11.46am the *Jean Bart* counter-attacked, forcing the *Augusta* to turn away sharply to avoid her salvoes at a range of 13 miles.

Within a few minutes the *Jean Bart* paid dearly for her initiative, receiving nine 1,000lb bombs that opened up enormous cavities in her deck. The Americans continued to dominate the air, destroying 12 French aircraft and attacking the heavy batteries at Casablanca. Unloading continued at an increasing pace with the use of Fedala harbour; and advancing American troops steadily infiltrated into strategic positions round Casablanca, while waiting for the arrival of the General Sherman tanks that had been put ashore at Safi.

Casablanca still held out, in spite of Admiral Darlan's broadcast that day, 10 November, calling on all French forces in North Africa to cease resistance. An all out American combined, sea, land, and air attack was therefore planned for 7.15am 11 November. In expectation, however, of French capitulation, orders were given that the assault should cease immediately if word were received that French resistance had stopped. It is noteworthy that the heavy covering bombardments by the American warships played an important part in the negotiations for an armistice.

At 6.00am on the 11th the flagship *Augusta*, the battleship *New York*, the AA cruiser *Cleveland*, and destroyers, got under way to take part in the final assault on Casablanca, but in less than an hour the cease fire order was given. At Fedala that afternoon General Patton and Admiral Hewitt for the Americans, and General Nogues and Admiral Michelier for the French, agreed that naval and military hostilities should be suspended.

There is an irony in the fact that with the end of the hostilities in which the US Navy had played such a crucial part and suffered comparatively little damage, misfortune should arrive in the shape of Axis submarines. On that same day on which hostilities ceased, *U273* sank a transport and damaged two other ships, and the following day *U130* sank three more transports A further transport was torpedoed on the 15th. Moreover although all harbour facilities were placed at the disposal of the Americans their use initially was greatly handicapped by the presence of 13 sunken ships.

On 17 November, Centre Attack Group's work having been completed, it sailed for the United States for follow-up operations. Rear-Admiral Hall was thereupon left in command of the Naval Operating Base at Casablanca.

The Assaults on Bougie and Bone

The Allied intention in operation Torch, was to race for Tunis and Bizerta as soon as troops and equipment had been put ashore at Algiers. Although Cunningham had strongly advocated a landing at Bizerta, the Allies had decided that the simultaneous assaults must be restricted to the three principal venues already considered in view of the severe limitation of resources. It would not be practical to land on D-day anywhere east of Algiers; not even with a small force. It was firmly believed however, that if the first troops to reach Tunis were those of the Allies, however few, the French there would swing over to the Allies, and welcome them.

Land communications east of Algiers were not sufficient to meet the 1st Army's needs for a rapid advance; i.e. if it were to be supplied only from Algiers. It had accordingly been planned that there should be additional assaults on the more easterly harbours of Bougie and Bone, (See Map 2, page 37), respectively 100 miles and 225 miles eastward of Algiers. These landings could not take place before D + 1 and were therefore planned for 9 November.

The object of the assault at Bougie (Operation Perpetual) was not only the occupation of an advanced assault base, but also the capture of the strategically placed airfield at Djidjelli at the same time. Though planned for 9 November, in the event the operation had to be postponed for two days because of bad weather and heavy surf on the beaches.

However, at 6.30pm on 10 November a fast 15 knot convoy of LSIs comprising the *Karanja, Marnix,* and *Cathay* left Algiers Bay for Bougie with the 36th Infantry Brigade Group already assault-stowed. A strong covering force consisted of the cruiser *Sheffield* (flying the flag of Rear-Admiral C. H. J. Harcourt), the 15-inch monitor *Roberts*, the auxiliary AA ship *Tynwald*, 5 destroyers, 5 corvettes, and half a dozen minesweepers, so that adequate strength for the bombardment of shore batteries would be available if required, though by then opposition was not expected. A slow convoy preceded them, carrying motor transport and supplies. In the *Karanja* were Captain N. V. Dickinson in charge of landings, and the military force commander Brigadier A. L. Kent-Lemon. Soon after 11.00pm they were followed by the *Awatea* another LSI, but bound for Djidjelli, carrying petrol and RAF Servicing Commandos who were to undertake servicing, refuelling, and re-arming as soon as the soldiers had captured the airfield at Djidjelli.

By 4.30am on 11 November the three landing ships were approaching the release position four miles off shore. Surf was heavy on the beaches and many landing craft got stranded. The *Sheffield* had closed right in under the guns of the fort at Cape Buac, below the limit of depression of the battery's guns. The *Roberts* prepared to bombard, screened meanwhile by an anti-submarine corvette and the AA cruiser *Tynwald*. There was, however, no opposition from the French, who thereupon gave permission in due course for the ships to close the harbour for unloading which was resumed at 10.00am. The slow convoy followed them in.

due to lack of air cover, including the *Karanja*, *Cathay*, and *Tynwald*.

'Bougie was full of survivors from the ships, but I am glad to say that, although *Awatea* was sunk soon after we left her with most of our stores, my Petty Officer reported later that we had suffered no casualties, and no loss of arms and ammunition, and that we were ready for action. While *Karanja* was on fire before sinking, some of my men commandeered a landing craft, went alongside *Karanja* and collected our stores.

'Bougie was indeed a nightmare, and we were more than pleased when we sailed from there in LCMs carrying petrol for the aircraft grounded at Djidjelli.'

An even more graphic account follows: this was extracted from notes, covered with oil fuel in places and almost illegible, written by Mr C. L. Harrand, serving at that time in the Hunt class destroyer *Bicester*.

'*10 November*
1530 Completed oiling and pushed off, went to Action Stations immediately. Several large transports are moving to sea with a destroyer escort. Aircraft carrier *Avenger* is with us. Sharp raid – bombs dropped close to *Avenger* – we didn't fire.
1800 We had expected escorting the convoy back to Gibraltar but we've set an easterly course, anchored again to wait for SS *Awatea* who is delayed in harbour.
2200 Steaming east at 22 knots with transport – no zig-zag; we must be in a hurry.
11 November
0530 (dawn) Action Stations – we are now inshore off Djidjelli – we were to cover the landing of troops here but for some unknown reason we are ordered to return west.
0800 Arrived at Bougie, other transports already there, port is in our hands. *Bicester* commences patrol outside harbour with other destroyers. Enemy aircraft are expected but haven't shown up.
1200 All forenoon quiet – destroyers still patrolling – two red warnings but no activity.
1310 The fun starts! Heavy air raid, flight of high flying bombers first – bombs dropping all around but no hits – miraculous how they miss – the barrage is tremendous.
1330 Sàvoia torpedo bombers approach and press their attack right inside the harbour – we are using a lot of ammunition.

Meanwhile, further eastward, the LSI *Awatea*, carrying petrol and RAF stores, had arrived off Djidjelli at the eastern end of the Gulf of Bougie, 30 miles from Bougie, only to find that a heavy swell made landing impracticable. She was accordingly ordered to return westward and unload at Duff White Beach in Bougie Bay where the swell was only slight. This change of plan had far reaching effects, for although Bougie was occupied without opposition, and the airfield at Djidjelli was later taken by paratroops, no petrol reached the airfield until the forenoon of 13 November. The ships and troops at Bougie and the Djidjelli airfield were therefore unable to have the intended Spitfire air cover, for the long period from noon on 11th until the morning of the 13th, and received very heavy bombing attacks by Axis planes. Limited cover was meanwhile provided by FAA fighters from the *Argus* and the *Avenger*, demand from whom was already extensive and who were themselves the objects of potential attacks. Hurricanes and Spitfires from Maison Blanche at Algiers provided some cover limited by the fact that they were operating at a radius of action of 100 miles from their fuelling and arming base. The Allies at this time had no operational airfield east of Maison Blanche.

The situation is described by Lt-Cdr M. V. Redshaw, VRD, RNR of the Royal Naval Commando 'G': 'We embarked in *Awatea* in company with the 5th Buffs for the next landing, which was at Bougie.

'The Bougie landing was no trouble, but this time the Luftwaffe and the Italian Air Force were organised, and for the best part of a week we had one big air raid, broken only by short intervals. During this week we helped discharge the follow-up store ships in the bay. We had no air cover during this period. (Our own air force being grounded at Djidjelli airfield awaiting the arrival of the petrol and ammunition that we were trying to get out of the ships in Bougie Harbour). Many ships were lost during this week

1340   One Savoia shot down on the beach. One Spitfire crashed on the hillside – all the torpedoes missed but some were very near.

1630   Several light attacks during the afternoon – bombers remain high and can't hit anything. Our job is to escort *Awatea* back to Algiers tonight.

1800   We had just got under way with the *Awatea* when a very heavy attack started – every gun in the harbour is firing – Ju 88s are attacking from all sides – the harbour is a mass of spray and columns of smoke. We are manoeuvring at full speed – dodging one after another. HMS *Wilton* is hot on starboard quarter. Low cloud is giving good cover for the attackers. Heinkels, Junkers 88s and 87s, and Focke Wulf 190s dive out of the cloud – drop bombs and disappear again. We have no fighter support.

1830   We have just had a very near miss, nearly bowled over by the blast. Torpedo carriers are attacking very low and close as the light fails – the barrage looks like a firework display.

1835   *Awatea* is hit by a bomb in her main hold, then immediately afterwards, by a torpedo in her port side. She catches fire and lists to port. Her after gun is still firing.

1900   The attack is over. *Awatea* is blazing like a torch in the darkness and we are closing in to render assistance. We pick up 25 survivors out of the water, some of them in a bad condition. The rest of her crew were leaving her, in lifeboats. It's now very dark and enormous flames are coming from her, making us all good targets. She is listing badly to port and we rig our hoses and approach her on her starboard side, but a corvette gets there before us and we back astern. Our captain decided to go under her port side. We are in an extremely dangerous position – close alongside her red-hot plates playing hoses on her – she is hanging over us at an alarming angle; suddenly she lurches a bit further and her davits foul our bridge and we sustain a lot of superficial damage. Flames reach right over our heads, and tremendous showers of sparks fly up as ammunition explodes inside her. She might go up at any minute and we should go with her. We stayed there for about 20 minutes then

withdrew and stood off. Shortly afterwards a tremendous explosion set her alight from end to end, there's nothing more we can do.

2200   We have returned to harbour and dropped anchor to await fresh orders – the survivors are taken ashore. Our ammunition situation is rather bad and the starboard Oerlikon is out of action – damaged alongside *Awatea*.

2315   We were heaving in anchor to go on patrol outside harbour when the 15,000 ton *Cathay* burst into flames amidships – probably a delayed action bomb from the earlier action. All hands on her quickly abandon ship – she is carrying a lot of ammunition and it's exploding all the time. She is alight from stem to stern – what a sight!

12 November

0700   We've been patrolling across the harbour entrance all night, the *Awatea* has capsized and foundered in deep water. The *Cathay* has lit up the sky for miles around, all night.

0715   Action Stations. Two Ju 88s attack out of cloud, one scores a direct hit on the *Karanja*, 18,000 tons. In a few seconds she is badly on fire. Our luck has changed with a vengeance now. A destroyer inshore is hit and sinks rapidly. We rush to *Karanja* to help, and again we pick up some badly injured men out of the water, then help to fight the fire. If the enemy come over now, we are a sitting target – there are no fighters.

A hell of a day. At 1000 we saw a very large flight of heavy friendly bombers pass over escorted by Spitfires – this cheered us up immensely. We cruised around trying to help *Karanja* till 1100 – then she was abandoned – the *Cathay* rolled over and settled in shallow water – that's about 45,000 tons of shipping burnt out in less than 24 hours. At 1100 we were attacked by Ju 88s, Stukas, Focke Wolfe 190s, and He 111s – a mass raid. We've little ammunition and no air support. We had to twist and turn at high speed to put them off their aim. Junkers are having it all their own way – no Spitfires. Fifteen bombs were dropped around us all together – we were very lucky. After an hour of continuous action we were hit aft – a small bomb struck X gun and started a fire – it is soon under control and we are still steering. At 1215 the attack was broken off and we turn to help the wounded. One officer and seven men killed and about seventeen others wounded. God – what a mess!

1230   We close inshore for instructions and are told to try to escort the *Marnix*, back to Algiers. We got under way and proceeded to sea at once. We are praying for a quiet time. *Bicester* is the only escort vessel, no 4-inch ammunition, little pompom; X gun and starboard Oerlikon out of action. At 1400 we received message from Bougie – "We are being attacked by about 50 Junkers" – so we have just missed another packet. The forward messdeck is like a shambles – dead and wounded lying on tables and deck. Everybody is dirty and hungry – several men whose nerves have cracked are being treated for shock. The doctor is working like a hero – performing operations, we all lend a hand where we can.

2000   Moored alongside the *Bulolo* at Algiers – no further trouble during the trip back. The wounded are

Right: *Glenfinlas* sunk alongside at Bougie on 13 November 1942.

taken ashore and the dead sewn up in canvas. We are here for the night.'

But much needed relief was at hand. Early on 13 November RAF Spitfires were operating from Djidjelli airfield. When the enemy next attacked shipping off Bougie on 14 November 11 raiders were shot down and many others damaged.

The absence of French opposition to the landings at Bougie was encouraging. A small mobile column known as Hart Force (a detachment of the 5th Northamptons, 11th Infantry Brigade) thereupon set off by road from Algiers for Bone. And at 3.00am on 12 November, the 6th Commando and two companies of the 3rd Battalion Royal West Kents were put ashore at Bone by the Hunt Class destroyers *Lamerton* and *Wheatland*; and two companies of the British 3rd Parachute Battalion were dropped at Bone at about the same time. The port and airfield were quickly captured. Mr J. E. Major, the navigator of a Dakota squadron, refers to his squadron delivering 500 gallons of petrol, per aircraft, in leaking non-returnable two gallon cans, to the airfield at Bone on 13 November. 'A somewhat hairy landing after dark', he comments, 'The only lights being a few hand-held torches. Much of the petrol we took in was used to replenish the American P-38 Lightnings that escorted us.'

The swift arrival of Axis forces at Bizerta and Tunis at this juncture however, now ruled out the feasibility of early occupation of those two strategic places by Allied airborne troops. British photographic reconnaissance on the 10th had revealed that 120 enemy aircraft, bombers, fighters, and transports, had already arrived at the Tunis airport of El Aouina; and the Sidi Ahmed airport at Bizerta was also in German hands. By 14 November Spitfires of the RAF 81 and 111 Squadrons had arrived at Bone, together with maintenance crews, petrol, and ammunition. But Axis air forces were by then reacting vigorously and on that day four Spitfires were destroyed on the ground. The primary aim of the Luftwaffe was to slow down the Allied advance while Axis land forces built up in Tunisia.

The original Allied plan provided for the rapid advance of British forces eastward, and General Anderson was anxious to implement this. After occupying Setif and Constantine, British troops had reached Tabarka a small port only 60 miles from Bizerta. They met steadily worsening difficulties due to lack of transport and torrential rain which ruined roads and airfields. Despite these highly adverse features they reached Mateur and Djedeida, less than a score of miles from Bizerta and Tunis, before being forced to fall back through lack of reinforcement and supplies. But that is another story of endurance and courage in the face of misfortune and the relentless rain that bogged down transport and men in entangling quagmires.

Bone proved to be a useful port with several unloading berths. It was also within the range of British cruisers and destroyers operating against the Axis supply ships that plied between Italy and Tunisia. For the destruction of these vessels Cunningham formed Force Q under the command of Rear-Admiral Harcourt. He also brought forward from Gibraltar to Bone, to be in charge of this vital port, Commodore G. N. Oliver in whose drive and competence he had great faith. In this easterly position the Germans had local air superiority; air attacks on the port occurred every night and day during November. Despite the heavy losses Cunningham was determined that Bone should be maintained as a forward base. Its retention was well justified in the light of subsequent events. The large LSIs could not be risked further east than Algiers. But the Algerian roads and railways were so limited and congested that coastwise shipping had to be used for sending reinforcements and supplies to Bone, usually at night. For this essential duty the medium sized transports the *Queen Emma, Prinses Beatrix, Royal Ulsterman*, and *Royal Scotsman* performed valiant service, always under air attack and sometimes threatened by U-boats, yet they came through triumphantly.

The part played by British submarines in the Mediterranean, has not always received adequate comment, and it is appropriate here to recall the Admiralty's message which expressed 'admiration for their tenacity and ingenuity in maintaining their offensive'. Despite long hours of routine patrol, in this case in wait for ships of the Italian fleet off the north-west corner of Sicily, submarine P 46, later named *Unruffled*, scored a hit on the Italian cruiser *Attilio Regolo*, on 8 November, which so badly damaged her that she had to be towed into Palermo. Her Captain, Lieut J. S. Stevens, (now Captain, DSO, DSC), writes: 'As soon as our last torpedo had been fired, we were on our way to the depths. ... Three escorts counter-attacked us for 1½ hours, dropping 40 depth charges. ... It was frustrating to have stopped and crippled a cruiser without the means to finish her off.' But *Regolo* was unable to take any further active part in the war.

One of the great problems for the uninitiated was that of correct identification; that is the recognition of friend from foe. There is nothing more lamentable than the destruction of friendly aircraft or friendly submarine. Captain P. J. Cowell, DSC, who was at that time Submarine Staff Officer, borne in the submarine parent ship *Maidstone*, comments: 'Our submarines were now switched from being a net round the Italian fleet, to offensive patrols on the German and Italian supply lines to Tunisia. They did a lot of damage, but we lost a lot of submarines. Fortunately some of their ship's companies fetched up in the bag.

'The French submarines were sent to patrol off the south of France and Corsica where they achieved very little except for *Casablanca* who when she had escaped from Toulon did very good and daring work. My biggest task was to try to keep our Air Forces clear of our submarines while at the same time letting them get at the enemy U-boats. Neither the American Air Force nor the French submarines were very good at understanding British methods.'

Captain G. A. Dukes, RE, who was in charge of a section of a Port Operating Company, had sad memories of Bone, and also refers to the danger from 'own weapons'.

'For a start, life was a little unpleasant at Bone', he writes. 'There was a shuttle service of bombers from Italy, and then we suffered our first casualties, among them the colonel and the adjutant. The *Aurora* did her best to discourage bombers, but we were thankful when a Z battery came along, together with some of my former gunner friends.

'Since every ship in the port opened up with its guns, we were perhaps in danger more from our own weapons than the enemy bombs. Certainly the low trajectory of some of the tracer was rather worrying. So much so that my section sergeant-major insisted on taking over the Oerlikon in one ship in which he was working. As he was a former heavyweight boxer (ex Guardsman Leek) nobody argued with him.'

One person who looked on the 'brighter' side of life in Bone was Captain P. M. B. Chavasse, CBE, DSC. 'On arrival in Bone', he writes, 'I found that the dock area was being heavily bombed. There was a mad Port Paymaster who had set up his office in the dock area. When I found it, the building was already extensively damaged. I thought that this was too good a chance to miss so I drew a £10 "casual". Much to my surprise, the office was still standing

next day but had suffered further damage. I drew another £10 "casual". These two payments caught me up about a year later.'

The story of Torch is full of misfortunes and delays experienced in obtaining petrol or supplies of ammunition or transport. The amazing thing is that it all worked out so successfully, through painstaking planning and sticking as far as possible to schedule, so that events could be properly co-ordinated. One can only pause for deep thought and admiration when realising the vastness of the operation. Perhaps the saddest feature was the intolerable and unremitting rain that slowed progress in the beginning and then for months obstructed movement practically altogether. The sadness is reflected in a soldier's brief note. 'I went ashore at Algiers', writes Mr T. G. Childerhouse, 'with the 2nd Bn Hampshire Regiment a few days after the initial landings; and without a pause we entrained in those almost historic French rail waggons, marked "8 Chevaux" or "40 hommes", for Tunisia and "Blade Force".

'By the end of November, and within sight of Tunis, my Battalion came under heavy counter attacks from the German armour which had been air-lifted to North Africa from Italy, and, as you probably recall, by December 3rd "The Hampshires" ceased to exist as a fighting force.'

Perhaps little enough credit has been given to the Royal Air Force in arriving in good time at newly seized airfields. Some of the many problems, gallantly surmounted, may be realised from a few comments in the following letter from Mr Nigel Gibbs: 'I was a navigator of a Beaufighter aircraft attached to No 89 Squadron. We were a night fighter squadron equipped with MK IV AI radar.

'One morning, we received instructions for six aircraft to proceed on detachment to Malta. Each aircraft was to be self-sufficient in stores and maintenance and we took off carrying, in addition to full ammunition load, a host of spare parts together with a Corporal fitter (airframe) and a fitter (engines). My pilot, Flg Off John Etherton had recently come across a large china wash basin in the desert near Tobruk. Despite the fact that this was devoid of any fittings in the way of taps or plugs, he considered that using it brought a certain degree of civilisation to life in the desert so we took this along as well.

'We refuelled at Malta and were then instructed to fly at wave-top level to Algiers to provide night air cover for the invasion force. We duly arrived in Algiers. But as we had been told we were going to Malta, we were still in open necked shirts and shorts. The pouring rain, ice-cold conditions, and lack of any appropriate clothing was a somewhat salutary shock. We operated from Maison Blanche originally, moving up later to Souk-el-Arba. Refuelling was carried out by hand from 6-gallon cans.

'As it was raining, quite a lot of water got into the tanks and we experienced a double engine cut due to water in the carburettors, at 500ft, after returning from the first patrol. We crash-landed on the edge of the aerodrome delivering a shock to some support army gunners as all our cannons went off as we hit the ground. Ignoring the

pointed remarks that it was supposed to be the other side we were there to destroy, we took off in another aircraft and succeeded in destroying an He 111.

'The detachment remained in North Africa for about six weeks. John Etherton and I achieved a personal score of six destroyed (including three in one night). The detachment's score was about 24. The ground crews did a magnificent job under the most difficult conditions and kept the aircraft airworthy despite the fact that each aircraft was doing about three patrols of 2½ hours each night. One of them, Cpl Rees, was awarded the George Medal for driving away a blazing petrol tanker from a Beaufighter during a ground strafing raid. As I was in the Beaufighter at the time, I was very well placed to appreciate his action. Most of the detachment received DFCs. Three of the six crews were killed.'

Great credit is also due to the Fleet Air Arm crews which were based on the aircraft carriers; and their readiness at all times to put up fighters, bombers, and reconnaissance aircraft, without regard to the hazards. The presence of the carriers in these waters was in itself a great risk, and the fact that not one was lost, with the exception of the *Avenger*, torpedoed when homeward bound, 15 November, must be accounted a great success for the never ending anti-submarine and anti-aircraft patrols.

A glimpse of the great demands on the time and skills of the medical fraternity is revealed in a description given earlier in this chapter of heavy bombing episodes. The extract that follows below, from a letter by Lt-Col B. C. Vaughan, RASC, and referring to the outward passage to Algiers shows a not uncommon, but less publicised venture to which the medical man may sometimes be called:

'Our passengers included a very large number of the staff of HQ First Army and the Lines of Communication, also most of Blade Force. (17th/21st Lancers part of 26th Armoured Brigade of 6th Armoured Division.) The Commander, Blade Force was on board, Colonel Richard Hull, now Field Marshal Sir Richard Hull. He had commanded the 17th/21st Lancers and had recently been appointed second in command of the Armoured Brigade.

'We had many senior army medical officers on board but apparently none qualified, or probably sufficiently practised to carry out an appendicitis operation. A private soldier was taken ill during the voyage and the Royal Navy

was asked for help. Our large troop ship was therefore stopped and a frigate or corvette put a Surgeon Lieutenant RNVR into a small boat to row across to us. A rope ladder was put down and with great difficulty the surgeon started to climb. He was half way up when his uniform cap fell off and it was fielded by one of the ratings. He promptly went down the ladder to get his cap, climbed the ladder again and landed on deck properly dressed as befitted a Naval Officer. The troop ship was stationary for over half an hour whilst he operated. After the operation he went back to his ship to the very loud cheers of the many hundreds of Army personnel on board. He undoubtedly saved the life of that soldier who I personally saw being disembarked on a stretcher at Algiers a few days later very happy and cheerful.'

Finally, a word is necessary on the relationship between the British and the Americans. Though speaking roughly the same language, the two nations had very different attitudes. The fact that in spite of the great difference in upbringing, there developed a tolerance amounting in due course to mutual respect and admiration, is nothing short of a miracle. It must be remembered that at this time the Americans had had little experience of action. The position is touched on in an extract from a letter by Mr F. C. Masters who was serving as Senior Assistant Purser of the transport *Mooltan* bound for Oran.

'I think the things that impressed us most were the complete unawareness of the Americans as to what war could be like and the amount and quality of their equipment. Whatever they had was in abundance and I can well recall the amazement of our own permanent British OC Troops when he saw the equipment and stores being loaded.

'Our captain, who was a "square-rigged" sailor, and was most punctilious in his dress and behaviour was completely shattered during our first action stations practice after sailing.

'The Americans had been allocated certain guns as reserve crews and it was decided to have a trial run and that we would put up some smoke shells for the Oerlikon gunners to fire at. The captain came from his day cabin on to the bridge and thence on to the wing of the bridge only to be confronted by an American soldier swinging back on the strap of his gun and blazing away; with an enormous cigar in the corner of his mouth. It required several pink gins and the assurances of the American OC Troops to restore him to his normal genial self. I think that at the moment he would have been capable of depositing said soldier over the side himself.

'The cigar smoking on the most unlikely of occasions was a source of wonder and amusement to us all as was the lack of formality between ranks, but in fairness it must be said that things seemed to get done; and when punishment was handed out it was usually fairly stiff from our point of view.'

The Political Battle and Follow-Up

We have seen that at Algiers there was resistance, particularly from the French Navy, almost throughout D-day, 8 November. Hostilities then ceased at 7.00pm that day when General Juin, representing Admiral Darlan, agreed that Allied Forces should occupy the city. The next morning, 9 November, the *Bulolo* entered harbour and berthed alongside, receiving an enthusiastic welcome from the populace.

At Oran on the other hand, there had been fighting all day on 9 November and the French had not capitulated until noon on 10 November when Admiral Darlan's cease-fire message had been broadcast.

At Casablanca fighting had continued until 6.55am on 11 November, and the ceasefire order was received only just in time to stop the American final assault on the city.

Meanwhile at Gibraltar there was relief at the news of the satisfactory way in which the occupation of Algiers and Oran was taking place, but some anxiety at the lack of news concerning the Western Task Force at Casablanca. It was known only that the French were putting up a stubborn fight there. Light bombers were sent off from Gibraltar to get in touch with the American commanders. These bombers were, according to Cunningham, shot down by French fighters or, more tragically, by American fighters who failed to recognise them. Cunningham then sent the fast cruiser-minelayer *Welshman* on 12 November after she had embarked Rear-Admiral Bieri, USN, to make contact with Hewitt at Casablanca.

'On the day of the landings', writes Cowell, the Submarine Staff Officer, 'I was twiddling the knobs on the radio in my office, when I picked up the Army intercom of the Americans at Casablanca. All seemed very depressing. I went up to lunch in the ward room and asked the staff if they had any better news. The reaction was instant as I was the only person with any news at all. Within minutes my office was full of top brass, Eisenhower and all.'

It is necessary to look back at the uncertain attitude of the French commanders. From the beginning of the Allied landings there was much vacillation among the French leaders, accompanied by acute suspicion and mistrust of the intentions of the Vichy government under Marshal Petain. The Marshal had taken over with great authority as head of state in unoccupied France in 1940. It should be realised that two years of Axis propaganda and promises had brought about uncertainties, and perhaps a diminishing faith in the name of the ageing Petain. Frenchmen ranged in opinion from that of the 'Free French' sponsored in Britain by General de Gaulle, to that of dedicated collaborators with the Germans. In general the French showed a loyalty to Petain and the chain of command, and this applied particularly in their regard for Admiral Darlan. They seemed however, lukewarm towards General Giraud. Despite the secret talks in North Africa arranged by Mr Murphy in October, which had been attended by Major-General Mark Clark, and the hope that had then prevailed that the Americans at least would be welcome as saviours in French Africa, the position remained obscure. The French generals and French admirals who favoured the Allies, were careful not to show too much readiness in supporting them. The matter was greatly complicated by other circumstances, a most important one being the knowledge that the Germans had secret plans in minute detail (Operation Attila), for the seizure of that part of France as yet unoccupied, together with the French fleet at Toulon. It was fairly certain that such an assault would be implemented if the Allies occupied North Africa. It should be noted also that Darlan had promised in 1940 that no part of the French fleet would fall into Axis hands. Their fleet in Toulon at the beginning of the Torch landings was substantial, and comprised a battleship, two battle cruisers, seven cruisers, 24 destroyers, 16 submarines, and small craft: a great prize which the Allies ventured to hope might fall into their own hands if the French were to join forces with the Allies.

On D + 1, 9 November, General Clark had flown to Algiers with Cunningham's Chief of Staff, Commodore Royer Dick, for talks with the French, as again arranged by Mr Murphy. Giraud stubbornly adhered to his plea that he must be created C-in-C of all the French forces in North Africa. Since it was obvious that he lacked local support, little progress was made.

But in the morning of 10 November, by which time Algiers was in the hands of the Allies (and Oran almost so), a meeting was held with Darlan and Juin which ended in the former signing an order for a general cease-fire throughout French North Africa. The atmosphere was tense. American troops were posted in the grounds round the Hotel St Georges; French naval guards had already been posted inside.

A request by Giraud to Darlan for a conference between them was at first rejected by the latter. It eventually was held in the afternoon of the 10th. Giraud then deplored the cease-fire signal made that morning by Darlan. He also insisted that he himself should be appointed C-in-C. By this time Darlan had received word from Marshal Petain that he, Darlan, had been officially discredited, and his cease-fire order was not valid. Darlan, by now thoroughly dejected, informed General Clark and Mr Murphy that he would revoke the cease-fire order, to which Clark then responded saying Darlan must be placed under house arrest to prevent this. Clark also suggested that Darlan should order the French fleet to sail from Toulon to Algiers so as to be beyond Hitler's grasp. Darlan replied that he was now in no position to do this. And so this wretched wrangle continued, valuable time being lost as the Germans prepared to seize that territory in Tunisia so tenuously held by the French.

It was early on the 11th that news reached Darlan that the Germans were moving into unoccupied France. This fact placed a different complexion on the matter. Darlan reasoned that Petain was no longer a free agent and that the Germans had broken the Armistice. He thereupon upheld the cease-fire agreement with the Allied leaders, strongly supported by General Juin, and made a signal to Admiral de la Borde, the C-in-C of the French fleet at Toulon, inviting him to sail the fleet direct to West Africa, and declaring that there would be no opposition from Allied naval forces.

The reply from de la Borde was an uncompromising

refusal, said to be expressed in one extremely unparliamentary French word.

Eisenhower and Cunningham at Gibraltar were of course being kept informed of the progress or otherwise of negotiations, and understood from Commodore Dick that Darlan was certain that the French fleet would not join the Allies. 'I'm afraid they will not come,' he is reported as saying.

By the afternoon of 11 November, (a fitting date for an armistice) local agreement was reached that Darlan should become the political head in French North Africa and Giraud the military commander of all the French forces, with Juin in command of the land forces. Prompted by a message from Cunningham, Darlan and Juin telephoned Admiral Esteva who was the Resident General of Tunis and an old friend of Cunningham, telling him to denounce the Axis and declare for the Allies. Cunningham sent a message to the effect that assistance would be rushed to him. It was however too late. The Germans were already flying into Tunis, and there was too much divided counsel to resist

Above left: General Giraud talking to French officials after his landing./*IWM*

Left: Amid the jeers of the local inhabitants 300 Italian prisoners were taken in lorries for embarkation in the docks. Soldiers and police acted as guards./*IWM*

Above: French Senegalese troops marching through the streets of Algiers./*IWM*

them in strength. Esteva replied to Darlan, 'I have a tutor at my elbow.'

A fortunate outcome of the local wrangles in Algiers was the release of almost a thousand British prisoners, including those who had been members of the ships' companies of the cruiser *Manchester* and the destroyer *Havock*.

Eisenhower and Cunningham flew to Algiers on 13 November for a long day of conference with the French leaders, preceded by a short meeting with Clark and Murphy. In brief, Eisenhower emphasised that the immediate object was to fight the Germans, and Darlan agreed. Cunningham deplored the delay in getting in touch with Esteva in Tunis, caused by Darlan's vacillation. Cunningham and Dick considered Darlan to be without scruple in pursuing the interests of his country. 'But', writes Dick, 'once decided on a course, in this case to work with the Allies, he carried out his engagements unswervingly'. Darlan was assassinated by a young fanatic on Christmas Eve 1942, and was given a State funeral which was attended by Eisenhower and Cunningham. Esteva, who was a true patriot and loathed the Germans, was eventually brought to trial in France in March 1945, and sentenced to imprisonment for life.

A complicating circumstance in the political tangle at Algiers was the fact that General de Gaulle had declared himself uncompromisingly for Britain in his support for the Free French. The new agreement between Eisenhower

and Darlan in Algiers therefore raised acrimony in both the British and American press. Eisenhower's contention was that he had no practicable alternative, other than to accept Darlan as a dependable ally.

Axis forces marched into unoccupied France on 14 November, declaring, as had Bonaparte in 1793, that they would not go so far as to occupy Toulon. Nevertheless this they did suddenly in the early hours of 27 November with intent to seize the French fleet. To prevent this, Admiral de la Borde was forced to scuttle most of his ships. A few of the smaller vessels were able to escape from the harbour, but of these only three submarines succeeded in reaching Allied ports. Of the ships scuttled one was a battleship, two were battle cruisers and seven were cruisers. The Admiral paid the price for his mistaken loyalty and local naval dissension, and was in due course sentenced to imprisonment for life.

Meanwhile Admiral Godfroy at Alexandria pursued a policy of studied vacillation. His fleet, which had been neutralised when he had come to an understanding with Cunningham in July 1940, comprised one battleship, four cruisers, and three destroyers, and for the moment were to remain idle at Alexandria.

Thus the great hope entertained by the Allies that French ships would join them in the struggle, failed to materialise. Nevertheless they could congratulate themselves on the success of the landings and the large measure of surprise achieved. On 22 November Clark and Darlan were able to sign an agreement mutually acceptable both to the Allies and to the French in North Africa, and on the following day it was announced that French West Africa would co-operate with the Allies. Thus, with the exception of Bizerta and Tunis, where they had been forestalled by the Germans, the Allies now held the whole coast of North Africa and West Africa from Tunisia to well down the West coast, including the valuable port of Dakar and many strategic airfields. With Anderson's 1st Army approaching Tunisia and being reinforced, and Montgomery's 8th

Above: Opening ceremony of Allied HQ at Algiers on 17 November 1942: (left to right) Clark (back view), Cunningham, Darlan and Anderson./*IWM*

Above right: Opening of Allied North African Headquarters. General M. W. Clark (American Army)./*IWM*

Right: The British and American flags are hoisted, while the French tricolour is hoisted by troops in centre./*IWM*

Army advancing rapidly through Libya to Tunisia, the strategic situation looked most favourable.

It needs to be stressed however at this point that the British 1st Army was not yet an army in the full sense of the word, comprising as it did one incomplete division and part of an armoured division. On 6 December it first became committed as the 5th Corps under Lieut-General C. W. Allfrey.

The assault convoy for Algiers had taken ashore the 78th Division (less one brigade group) with some AA units, and the advanced HQ of two RAF wings.

The follow-up convoy arrived at Algiers on 12 November. By that time ships were able to unload in the harbour. They carried the 1st Army's advanced HQ, and those of the Eastern Air Command, and an armoured regimental group of the 6th Armoured Division, called 'Blade Force', together with a parachute brigade.

Subsequently KMF and KMS convoys sailed from Britain at approximately 15 day intervals, and the empty transports returned home for further reinforcements. Similarly for the UGF and UGS convoys, though in their case the intervals were 25 days between sailings from USA.

After the initial landings there were several casualties among the transports, especially when proceeding unescorted, and the escorts themselves also suffered. Nevertheless, strategically the position had improved immeasurably. Malta was once again relieved by the fast minelayers *Manxman* and *Welshman*, and in its turn was now able to return to the offensive with FAA and RAF torpedo bombers, renewed submarine strength, and a

Above left: French soldiers at the ceremony unfurl the flag./*IWM*

Above right: Lieutenant-General K. A. N. Anderson, who commanded the British First Army, photographed at the ceremony./*IWM*

Left: Group of Officers at the ceremony. (Left to right) General M. W. Clark (US Army), Admiral Sir Andrew Cunningham (C-in-C Mediterranean), Lieutenant-General K. A. N. Anderson (Commanding First Army) and Admiral Darlan./*IWM*

resuscitation of Force K. All this in combination with the new Force Q operating from Bone, together with skilfully placed minefields, brought about increasing Axis losses, especially in the Italian supply routes to the Western Desert.

There is no place here for a blow by blow account of the Allied troops in their relentless progress eastward, and the various delays, setbacks, and misfortunes that were suffered. Suffice it to say that General Anderson wasted no time. Conscious of the rapid German build-up that had already begun in Tunisia, he decided on a move eastward by all available forces, in the hope that he would be able to attack Bizerta and Tunis in about a week's time. Accordingly on 15 November, advanced parties of the 11th Infantry Brigade Group and 'Blade Force' were directed on Souk-el-Arba through Souk Ahras; 'Hart Force' on Djebel Abiod; and the 36th Infantry Brigade Group on Tabarka, to be joined by its detachments from Bougie, Djidjelli, and Setif as soon as those troops were replaced by units of the 34th US Infantry Division. As we know from the previous chapter, his plans were frustrated and

his army bogged down by torrential rain and quagmires, while the Germans poured in troops and equipment with the advantage of proximity and local air superiority. But as Liddell Hart states in his *History of the Second World War*, 'A failure to gain immediate success has at times turned out very advantageously by helping towards fuller success and making final success more sure. . . . It was due to the Allies' original advance on Tunis from Algiers in November 1942, that Hitler and Mussolini were encouraged to send a stream of reinforcements there, across the sea, where the Allies were eventually able to trap them [about a quarter of a million troops] six months later, and put two Axis armies in the bag – thus removing the chief obstacle to their later jump from Africa into Southern Europe.'

It was to be 8 May 1943 that Cunningham would make his famous signal 'Sink, burn, destroy. Let nothing pass' to ensure that practically none of the Axis troops should escape by sea.

However, perhaps in the minds of those Allied seamen who had taken part in Operation Torch, Cunningham's signal of 14 November 1942, stands in greater memory.

'From: Naval Commander Expeditionary Force
To: All concerned in Operation Torch
'In my message to you before this operation started I called on you for all your efforts in a hazardous operation of supreme importance to our countries.
'The response has been all and more than I hoped and I thank captains, officers, and men alike, for the courage,

Above: North African operations. American General Grant tanks after being landed./*IWM*

Right: On the Tunisian battlefront. One of the American tanks (a Sherman - deleted by censor) after the battle, 11 December 1942./*IWM*

Below right: First pictures of fighting in Tunisia. A German tank smashed up in the battle near Tabourka./*IWM*

efficiency, and resolution with which they played their part.

'My pride in the work of the Merchant Navy, and the confidence that I have learnt to place in them after two years of hard warfare in the Mediterranean, have been proved yet again. This was my first contact with United States ships and I emphasise that this message applies with equal force to them in this operation.

'I send captains, officers, and crews my thanks, and wish them Godspeed.'

(Sgd) Andrew Cunningham
Admiral.'

Cunningham embarked the next day, 15 November in the cruiser *Aurora* at Gibraltar for a visit to Oran to inspect progress in the clearance and use of the port. Much work had yet to be done in removing wrecks so as to provide more accommodation for the unloading of transports. He also made arrangements for the berthing of the heavy ships of Force H at the naval port of Mers-el-Kebir. Though the Italian heavy ships had shown no sign of opposing the Allied landings their presence in their own harbours remained a potential threat, so that it was necessary that units of Force H should be retained in the Western Mediterranean.

In his official despatch Cunningham ended by paying a compliment to the Commander-in-Chief. 'It should be placed on record', he wrote, 'That in this most difficult of all types of operation with a number of services involved, and despite the difficulties inherent in welding together the systems of command and organisation, there reigned a spirit of comradeship and understanding which provided that vital force which brought success to our undertakings. The embodiment of that spirit was exemplified in our C-in-C, General Dwight D. Eisenhower: we count it a privilege to follow in his train.'

Some 2½ years later, Eisenhower in a letter to Cunningham, who was then First Sea Lord, wrote: '. . . the hours that you and I spent together in the dripping tunnels of Gibraltar will probably remain as long in my memory as

Top: A General Grant's gun has a pull-through after the capture of the village of Medjez-ej-Bab./*IWM*

Above: Beating the retreat for sunset at Oran./*H. B. Hamilton*

Above right: One of the Arabs helping the British Red Cross./*IWM*

will any other. It was there I first understood the indescribable and inescapable strain that comes over one when his part is done – when the issue rests with fate and the fighting men he has committed to action.'

Eisenhower left the dripping tunnels at Gibraltar on 24 November to move his headquarters to the Hotel St Georges in Algiers. He was followed the next day by Cunningham who occupied a villa in the same garden. Torch had been a complete and brilliant success at all the landing places in Africa. Not only were there substantial gains from the point of view of naval supremacy and air support for Allied shipping in the Atlantic, with a continuous air cover now possible from Gibraltar to Freetown, but there was the important prospect that the Mediterranean would soon be once more open for shipping from Gibraltar to Alexandria.

Chance plays some peculiar tricks and they are not always favourable. In this connection the following story by Rear-Admiral C. D. Howard-Johnston may be of interest:

'I had nothing really to do with Operation Torch being at the time merely on the Staff of C-in-C Western Approaches and concerned with A/S Operations.

'However, many of our units were being withdrawn for the operation which was all very secret. So much so that only the Chief of Staff and his assistant, Captain Bill Ravenhill, were allowed to see the orders. These were distributed in double envelopes with the outer envelope marked Bigot which was an Admiralty code word indicating that only certain named officers were allowed to open this outer envelope, and no one below the rank of captain.

'I was a commander at the time and one day while yarning with Bill Ravenhill I casually remarked, "Is this business going to happen off Gibraltar?" To my astonishment Bill Ravenhill, normally an exceedingly calm person, appeared to be electrified by my remark. He almost roared at me . . . "How the hell did you know?" I had merely noticed that Bigot, read backwards, indicated *To Gib*. Thereafter, there was much telephoning from the Chief of Staff to NID Admiralty where I understand the code word *Bigot* had been chosen from a list of words available. Not

being supposed to know anything about the operation I asked no more questions and heard nothing more.

'But it makes the point that a haphazard codeword can be a give-away! The rendezvous as you know being off Gibraltar.'

Quite apart from security, important lessons had been learned concerning the use and management of landing craft, and the vital need to have fighters in the air early enough and sufficient in strength to establish and maintain local air superiority. Perhaps for Cunningham the greatest regret was that the great gamble had not gone far enough. He remained convinced that a landing at Bizerta would have been not only practicable but successful, by bringing in the French there on the side of the Allies before the Germans could land in strength. His previous acquaintanceship with Admiral Esteva supported this view.

The lessons learned could now be put into practice for the next amphibious operation. The exact place for this was as yet unclear except that it would be somewhere in the 'soft underbelly' of the Axis. But the Torch had now been lit.

'Heaven doth with us as we with torches do,
Not light them for themselves;
For if our virtues did not go forth of us,
'Twere all alike as if we had them not.'

Measure for Measure,
Act I, Scene I.

Top left: All is lost for the two Axis armies in North Africa: General von Arnim arrives for the surrender in May 1943./*IWM*

Left: Allied flags are lowered as national anthems are played./*H. B. Hamilton*

Below: President Roosevelt and Mr Churchill meet in North Africa. (Left to right) General Giraud (High Commissioner for French North Africa), President Roosevelt, General de Gaulle (Leader of the Fighting French) and Mr Churchill, 24 January 1943./*IWM*